THE AMERICAN DREAM IN LEBANON, IRAQ, AND THE MIDDLE EAST

by

Dr. Bassam Hamdan

authorHOUSE®

AuthorHouse™
1663 Liberty Drive, Suite 200
Bloomington, IN 47403
www.authorhouse.com
Phone: 1-800-839-8640

This book is a work of non-fiction. Unless otherwise noted, the author
and the publisher make no explicit guarantees as to the accuracy of

First published by AuthorHouse 3/10/2008

ISBN: 978-1-4343-7337-3 (sc)

Library of Congress Control Number: 2008901929

Printed in the United States of America
Bloomington, Indiana

This book is printed on acid-free paper.

DEDICATION

The book is dedicated to the American and free-world soldiers who sacrificed and served in Lebanon, Iraq, and the Middle East. To all parents deprived of their children, to the orphans, and the wounded who are suffering on a daily basis from the savage consequences of the hate culture. Also to my professors at University of Alabama, Dr. Patricia Rudolph, Dr. Billy Helms, Dr. William Jeans, Dr. Walter Misiolek, Dr. Edward Mansfield, Dr. T. Martell, To every Christian, Muslim, and Jew. I say with them, we are fed up with the hate culture; we want peace and only peace.

Dr. Bassam Hamdan
PhD in Finance

"We hold these truths to be self-evident, that all men are created equal, that they are endowed by their creator with certain unalienable rights, that among these are Life, Liberty, and the Pursuit of Happiness."

<u>Source</u>: The Declaration of Independence of the United States of America. July 4, 1776.

CONTENTS

INTRODUCTION

Two hundred and fifty years ago, the immigrants to America were fighting the British army. Later on France moved in, hoping to get a share of the new world's wealth. Thousands died, tragic events happened, with heavy financial and social losses. Again, 150 ago, the American immigrants fought against each other in an ugly civil war. It increased the pain and agony of all involved. Also, sixty years ago, the Americans sent their kids to fight alongside the French and the British against the Nazis.

They ignored the tragic events and the suffering of their grandparents when they fought the British and the French seeking a free America. They ignored the past and participated in fighting Nazi Germany to guarantee freedom and dignity to Europe and the whole world. During the second world war, millions died, fortunes were lost, and cities and villages were destroyed. Many things happened in a short period of time. But the pain and agony led to drastic changes in the people's attitudes and beliefs. They do not believe in wars anymore. The question is, do you consider the Americans unfaithful to the memory of their parents because they helped the British and the French during the second world war? Moreover, after the war, the American people helped the Europeans and the Japanese rebuild their countries. Today the Euro land is a reality. Do you consider the French and German peoples unfaithful to their parents? No, the opposite is true. It is a normal thing to change. Man is kind and good by nature. Establishing peace between different cultures and religions is the true worship, because God is lord of forgiveness and love. This is the peace culture.

In the Middle East, there is a different culture, the hate culture. Religious discrimination and hate passed on from one generation to another with strong resistance to change. Nobody really knows where the Middle East, Iraq, Somalia, Sudan, and Lebanon are going. The new generation loves life, like all kids everywhere; they enjoy music, dancing, sports, and leisure time. Everyone is interested in having modern hospitals and universities.

Recently the trend toward peace culture became stronger. Well-educated people discuss it openly. As an example, a physician and a writer wrote an article in the Saudi newspaper *Al-Watan*, issue number

2607 dated Monday, November 19, 2007. She mentioned that one of the readers sent her an e-mail stating the following:

In a textbook used to teach religion to the third grade elementary students, it encourages the children to hate the Non-Muslims.

He questioned "Why they want me to hate the Jewish scientist who discovered the Insulin medication which benefited large number of patients including my mother? Do I have to teach my daughter to hate Edison, who invented the Electrical Lamp, which benefited everyone including the Muslims? Do I have to teach my daughter to hate the others simply because they believe in different religion? Why do we make our religion a religion of hate towards the others?

Unfortunately within days a Muslim clergy answered back in an article in the same newspaper, *Al-Watan*, issue number 2610 dated Thursday, November 22, 2007. He wrote,

There are several sections in the Quran such as - - - -, it state clearly that we should hate the infidels (Non-Muslims), do we reject it to accept the lady writer false opinion? - - - -.

This is just a simple example of the current confrontation between the hate culture followers and those who believe in the peace culture. It is strange; my father is Muslim and my mother is Christian. Does this mean that I have to hate my mother simply because she is Christian? She went to college sixty years ago and worked in the French army hospitals based in Lebanon during that period. Moreover, she received on December, 30, 1948 a Bronze Medal from the Lebanese president Bishara Alkhouri in appreciation for her efforts as a member in the Lebanese Red Cross medical mission during the 1948 war in Israel. She did sixty years ago what most of the Arab women hope to do today. She is my sweet, loving angel.

Luckily the peace culture is growing in some areas in the Middle East. In the universities and chambers of commerce there are new strong voices calling for peace. In Egypt the president, Hosni Mubarak, initiated new laws establishing special family courts to accelerate the process of solving cases of the abuse of children and women. Also, he appointed several well-known ladies as judges in the family courts.

Moreover, the judicial system made more of an effort to fight corruption by going after senior officials in the government. Also, the media and official government television paid more attention to covering prayers from the churches for long hours.

In the kingdom of Bahrain, the king personally follows up and supports the efforts to build new churches or expanding old churches.

The leaders of the United Arab Emirates and Kuwait pay attention to this issue also. More Arab leaders and intellectuals are trying hard to influence the current trend and to spread the peace culture in the Middle East. Are we going to succeed in achieving the American dream in every single country in the Middle East? I hope so.

CHAPTER ONE

Comparing the History of the USA and Lebanon

Lebanon, a small country on the Mediterranean, has total population of 4 million. The number did not change much over the years due to the continuous immigration of the Lebanese people to countries all over the world. Civil wars, corruption, religious discrimination, a high unemployment rate, inflation, lack of equal distribution of wealth: there is a long list of factors that lead to the continuous immigration of the Lebanese families. The Lebanese people did not enjoy real independence. In 2008, after sixty years of independence, the Lebanese people are still looking for the means to protect and support freedom and democracy in Lebanon. There are more than 15 million Lebanese immigrants outside Lebanon in the USA Canada, Europe, and all countries. The Lebanese immigrants seek the American dream of happiness, success, and stability. Outside Lebanon they live together in harmony and peace regardless of religion or sect. But inside Lebanon the religious conflicts never end. Is there any hope to end it? Any realistic solution? Is it possible to bring the American dream to Lebanon? This will provide the Lebanese families with an opportunity to achieve their hopes and the American dream without immigrating or leaving Lebanon. In other words, they would achieve the American dream in Lebanon and the Middle East.

The Lebanese political system carries the seeds of destruction because it allows the following practices:

1. Religious discrimination. Even in hiring government employees the new entrants are selected in sets. Every set includes one person from every religion or sect. So, when there is a qualifying exam or test for new job, if the top ten candidates are Christians, the first two persons who are accepted, one candidate ranked one (Christian) and candidate ranked eleven (Muslim) and so on.

   Obviously this led to a situation where the loyalty of the people is to their religious leaders, not to their homeland, Lebanon.

2. A small group of families and leaders in every religion and sect have a monopoly on the financial and economic resources in the country.

3. Corruption prevailed in all aspects of life—financial, administrative, economic, and health. This situation deprived the highly motivated entrepreneurs of equal opportunities to establish real, productive economic units and companies, which led to forcing the good, active entrepreneurs to go out of the country, seeking the American dream in the USA and in the free countries worldwide.

4. Weak judicial system. The courts and judges in general are controlled by politicians. Keep in mind that the politicians are grouped into religious and sectarian groups.

5. In most of the cases, the politicians are linked directly to foreign countries. Money and guns received from the foreign countries play an important role in shaping the Lebanese political scene.

6. Lack of safety and security in the country. Most of the politicians maintain armed groups of supporters using "personal safety" as an excuse.

Various countries suffered from wars and selfishness. But people learn and change, and at a certain point they move toward the peace culture. Human beings are peaceful by nature. The way one is raised, the concepts fed into his/her mind by the parents and teachers in school, and the pain or suffering one is subjected to through time shape his/her personality and behavior. Table 1 includes a comparison of the history of the USA and Lebanon. Kindly note that even though the Lebanese people live in a small geographical area and are of a limited population size, the religious discrimination and wars persist after thousands of years. The hate culture still dominates the country, while in the USA we see that immigrants from different countries with different languages, races, religions, and cultures managed to unite and merge together in one great nation over a period of three hundred years only, even though they had wars against the British, French, and the Mexicans. Also, they suffered from a civil war and several assassinations of American presidents. But all of these events did not prevent them from establishing the greatest and best country in the world. The immigrants succeeded in achieving this major achievement because they believed in great principles such as:

1. All citizens are equal regardless of their religion, race, or origin.

2. Freedom of thought and speech.

3. Fair distribution of wealth in the country. Best efforts being exerted by all to provide the people equal opportunities to have good education and work.

4. Establishing a land of laws. Best efforts are exerted by all to apply the same laws fairly and equally to every one. They accept the fact that every accused person is innocent until proved guilty in a court of law.

5. The right of having a good education for all.

6. Respect for minorities and the weak groups such as the children.

7. The right of every person to vote in the elections in the country.

8. Peaceful transfer of power to the elected group.

9. Freedom of the media and the press.

The idea of the American dream succeeded in providing happiness, security, freedom, and success to the people.

The American system succeeded in getting the best out of everyone through providing the people equal opportunities to get education, medical assistance, financing, legal assistance, and security. In short, it is a stable social, economic, and political environment. The immigrants from all over the world succeeded in building the modern American society, which enabled 300 million Americans to achieve a gross domestic product (GDP) in the year 2005 equivalent to 12.4 trillion U.S. dollars. This high level of productivity gave the American citizen the right and the opportunity to live comfortably—better than anyone else worldwide. It also provided the means to spend money on studies, research, and development in all areas, especially medicine, the space program, and modern technology, plus providing economic assistance to the needy worldwide.

In Lebanon and the Middle East, after thousands of years, we failed to build a modern country or society. Today, in 2008, Lebanon is close to civil war again, with the Lebanese people divided into separate religious groups. Unfortunately the whole Middle East suffers from similar problems. The total population of the Arab countries of 309 million generated a GDP in 2005 equivalent to 1031 billion U.S. dollars. Non-oil GDP equals approximately 600 billion U.S. dollars.

The hate culture and wars in the Middle East resulted in putting everything on hold. Oppression and ignorance prevailed; unjust treatment of the well-educated and skilled persons forced them out of the Middle East. This brain drain is the main loss. Whereas, in the USA, the liberty statue became symbol of human dignity and freedom. The USA continued to attract the motivated entrepreneurs and skilled people such as the computer programmers in recent years, which supported the American economy and generated billions of U.S. dollars.

Table 1
History of the USA and Lebanon

LEBANON			USA
EVENT	**DATE**	**DATE**	**EVENT**
Several kingdoms on the Mediterranean (SIDON, TYRE, BYBLOS, BEIRUT) known as the PHOENICIANS	3 0 0 0 BC		
The Egyptian pharaoh THUTMOSE III invaded Lebanon and Syria	1490– 36 BC		
Several independent kingdoms again	1 2 0 0 BC		
The Assyrians invaded the area (Lebanon and Syria).	8 7 5 – 608 BC		
The Babylonians invaded the area (Lebanon and Syria).	685–36 BC		
The Persians invaded the whole area (Lebanon and Syria).	539-38 BC		
Alexander the Great invaded the area (Greek influence). He died in 323 BC One of his officers, Seleucus-I, took over Lebanon.	333 BC		
The Roman Empire invaded the area (Lebanon and Syria).	64 BC		
The Roman Empire split into two parts: One part had Rome as the capital. The other one had the Byzantines with Constantinople as capital. The Byzantines ruled Lebanon.	AD 395		

LEBANON			USA
EVENT	**DATE**	**DATE**	**EVENT**
The Arab tribes spread Islam to the area.	632-34		
Muawiyah established the rule of the Umayyads in the area, with Damascus as capital.	660-750		
The sons of Prophet Mohammad's uncle, Abul Abbas, defeated the Umayyads and established the "Abbasids rule" and built the city of Baghdad, which would be the capital.	750		
Caliph Al-Hakim, head of the Fatimids of Egypt. They ruled the area.	9 9 6 – 1021		
The Crusades (eight campaigns) prevailed in the area.	1 0 9 5 – 1291		
The Mamluk Sultanate. The Turkoman slaves took over Muslim Ayyubid Sultanate in Egypt and ruled Egypt and the area in Lebanon	1 2 8 2 – 1516		
The Ottoman Turks Sultanate Sultan Salim-I defeated the Mamluks and invaded the area. <u>The MAAN family</u>	1 5 1 6 - 1916	1 4 9 2 Oct. 12	Columbus discovers the new world.
* Prince Fakhr ad Din I	1516-44	1498	Columbus, on third voyage discovers, South America.
* Prince Fakhr ad Din II (exiled to Tuscany: 1613-1618)	1 5 7 0 - 1635	1513	Ponce de Leon discovers Florida.

LEBANON		USA	
EVENT	DATE	DATE	EVENT
The SHIHABS Family * Prince Bashir II (allied himself with Muhammad Ali, ruler of Egypt)	1697-1842	1565	Founding of St. Augustine City, Florida.
		1579	Drake explores coast of California.
		1636	Harvard College founded.
		1639	The first constitution in America adopted by Connecticut
		1776, July, 4	Declaration of Independence
		Sept. 3 1783 - Nov. 25, 1783	Final treaty of peace is signed. British army evacuates New York.
*European Ambassadors (Britain, Austria, Prussia, and Russia) plus the Othmans worked together to push Muhammad Ali out of Lebanon and the area.	Sept. 1840	1790	First census, population 3,929,214
* Prince BASHIR II went into exile.	Oct. 4, 1840	1808	Prohibition of the foreign slave trade

LEBANON			USA
EVENT	DATE	DATE	EVENT
		1819	Purchase of Florida from Spain
* Prince Bashire III	Sept. 3, 1840	1828	Building of the first passenger railway began in Baltimore.
		1830	Fifth census, population 12,566,020
Double Qaimaqamate System Established two districts: Christian Northern District and Druze Southern District, with Beirut–Damascus highway partitioning the two districts	Dec. 7, 1842	1844	First telegraph line in America, between Baltimore and Washington
* Christian–Druze conflict	1845	1848	Discovery of gold in California
* Tanyus Shahin (Maronite Christian) revolution against the land lords.	1858		
* Christian–Druze conflict	1860		
* International commission of France, Britain, Austria, Prussia and the Ottoman Empire to analyze the 1860 conflict	Oct. 5, 1860		

LEBANON		USA	
EVENT	DATE	DATE	EVENT
Mustasarriffia Administration		1861, Feb. 4	Confederate government organized
Statue of 1961 Mount Lebanon		1865, Apr. 9	Surrender of Lee at Appomattox
* Lebanon separated from Syria	1861	1865, Apr. 14	Assassination of Lincoln, Andrew Johnson President
* Headed by non-Lebanese Christian (Mutasarriff) assisted by a council of twelve members representing the various religions.		1865, Apr. 26	Surrender of Johnston's army
The American University of Beirut founded	1866	1867	Purchase of Alaska
		1876	Invention of the telephone
		1876	Custer's army destroyed by the Indians
		1880	Population 50,155,783
The French St. Joseph's University founded	1875	1881	James A. Garfield inaugurated president
		1881, July 2	Assassination of Garfield; dies on September 19. Chester A. Arthur becomes president.
		1886, Oct. 6	Statue of Liberty unveiled, New York

LEBANON			USA
EVENT	**DATE**	**DATE**	**EVENT**
World War I	1914	1 9 0 1 , Sept. 6	President McKinly shot by an assassin; dies on Sept. 4. Theodore Roosevelt becomes president.
San Remo Conference in Italy. The Allies gave France a mandate over greater Syria (Syria and Lebanon).	April, 1920		
French General Gouraud announced the establishment Greater Lebanon with Beirut as the capital. The French general added to the Mutasarriffia of Lebanon the following cities: Beirut, Bekaa Valley, Tripoli, Sidon, and Tyre and made it one country, Greater Lebanon. The Muslims rejected the Greater Lebanon concept.	1 9 2 0 , Aug. 31.		
The first Lebanese constitution	1 9 2 6 , May		
First and only census in Lebanon till today	1932		
World War II • French Vichy government control • Free France General de Gaulle visited Lebanon.	1 9 3 9 - 1945	1 9 3 9 - 1945	World War II
General Georges Catroux proclaimed the independence of Lebanon.	1 9 4 1 , Nov. 26		
New chamber of deputies elected Bishra Al Khouri as president. He appointed Riyad as Sulh as prime ministers.	1 9 4 3 , Sept. 21		

LEBANON			USA
EVENT	DATE	DATE	EVENT
The chamber of deputies amended the constitution, abolishing the articles that referred to the mandate. Thus unilaterally ended the mandate. The French authorities arrested the Lebanese leaders and put them in the Castle of Rashayya.	1943, Nov. 8		
France released the prisoners. This day is considered the independence day.	1943, Nov. 22		
Lebanon joined the League of Arab States (Arab League).	1945, Mar. 22		
Lebanon joined the San Francisco conference of the United Nations (UN) and became a member.	1945	1945– 2007	• Economic development • Industrial development • Development of financial markets and institutions • Space program • Information and communication technology
French troops left Lebanon.	1946, Dec. 31		
Civil war (limited)	1958		
The good days of Lebanon	1958- 1975		
Civil War: • Christians-Muslims and Palestinians • Christians–Christians • Muslims–Muslims • Shia Muslims – Palestinians	1975- 1990		

LEBANON			USA
EVENT	**DATE**	**DATE**	**EVENT**
War with Israel	2 0 0 6 , July		
• Country is close to civil war again. • European ministers of foreign affairs (France, Italy, Spain) and USA officials; Dr. Umar Mousa, general secretary of the Arab League; and Mr. Moon, the general secretary of the United Nations, are working with the Lebanese leaders to help them elect a president. • Unfortunately in Lebanon history is repeated again and again.	2 0 0 7 , Nov.		

Source: http://www.lgic.org/
        http://workmall.com/
        Based on information from the Library of Congress country
        studies.

CHAPTER TWO

The Other Face of the Hate Culture

The political system in Lebanon, which is based on religious discrimination and corruption, resulted in the growth of the hate culture in the country. Unfortunately the same situation prevailed in the Middle East, which affected negatively the gross domestic product and the whole economy, as indicated by the statistics prepared by experts from the World Bank and the International Monetary Fund.

The gross domestic product of the Arab countries in year 2005 reached 1031.8 billion U.S. dollars. The non-oil GDP is approximately 600 billion U.S. dollars, which means that the GDP per capita is much less than that in other countries (Table 2).

Table 2
GDP and Population in Selected Countries

Country	Population (Millions)	Gross Domestic Product (Billion U.S. $)
Germany	82.5	2800
Japan	127.8	4500
Sweden	9.0	357.7
Austria	8.2	306.1
Denmark	5.4	258.7
Finland	5.2	193.0

Norway	4.6	295.5
Korea	48.3	791.4
USA	296.4	12400
Lebanon	4.0	21.5
The Arab Countries	309.4	1031.8

The low productivity level is a result of the hate culture, which lead to several wars (in modern history) such as:

- The civil wars in Lebanon (1958, 1975–1990)
- The Iraq-Kuwait war
- The Arab–Israel wars (1948, 1967, 1973, and 2006)
- The Western Desert (Sahara) war in Morocco
- The civil war in Sudan (South Sudan, Darfur)
- The civil war in Yemen
- The civil war in Jordan with the Palestinians (1970)
- The civil war in Somalia.
- Military uprisings in several Arab countries (Syria, Libya, Iraq, and Sudan)

Several countries worldwide suffered from wars that resulted in destruction of cities and the deaths of millions. But the agony and pain of the wars contributed to the emergence of the peace culture in the USA, Europe, and Asia.

The peace culture means less corruption, better education and social benefits to the people, and freedom and dignity for everyone. The USA spread the peace culture worldwide after the second world war, even in Germany and Japan, which explains the high productivity levels in both countries. So it is possible to increase the productivity of the Arab countries several times simply by moving toward the peace culture. This means that every Arab family in Lebanon, Syria, Jordan, Egypt, Yemen, Iraq, etc., will enjoy higher living standards and better social benefits.

The most important factor is having the will to change; next comes the ability to do it. Obviously reaching this goal requires full participation of the universities, research centers, and the media and government officials throughout the Middle East countries to educate the public and introduce the mechanism of managing the change process. It would be very difficult, but failing to do it means that life in the Middle East will be more difficult and worse for all involved.

In this regard I recommend as a starting point telling the public in Lebanon, Iraq, and the Middle East the details of the true current position of the Arab countries compared to the performances of other countries. Based on statistics from the World Bank and the International Monetary Fund, I prepared a summary of several indicators such as:

- Economical
- Educational
- Business environment
- Technological
- Environmental
- Privatization process
- Military expenditures
- Financial
- Enterprise surveys

Economic Indicators, Table 3
Comparing the data of the Arab countries with selected industrial countries

• Unemployment rate	: High
• Life expectancy	: Relatively lower (except the GCC countries, where it is high)
• Fertility rate	: High
• Mortality rate—infants (per 1000 child)	: High
• Mortality rate—Children under five (per 1000 child)	: High
• GDP	: Low
• Inflation rate	: High
• Agriculture, value added	: High
• Industry, value added	: Average to above average
• Services, value added	: Less than average

Country	Labor Force (Million)	Unemployment Rate (% of Labor Force)	Total Population (Million)	Population growth rate (annual %)	Life Expectancy at Birth (year)	Fertility Rate (Births per woman)	Mortality rate Infant (per 1000 Live Birth)	Mortality Rate Under 5 (per 1000)	GDP (Current US $ Billion)
ARAB COUNTRIES									
Bahrain	0.34	5.2 (2000)	0.73	N/A	N/A	N/A	N/A	N/A	N/A
Egypt	22.9	11	74	1.90	70.5	3.1	28.00	33.00	89.7
Iraq	8.3	26.8	24.4 (2000)	N/A	N/A	N/A	N/A	N/A	25.9 (2000)
Jordan	1.8	12.4	5.5	2.30	72.0	3.3	22.00	26.00	12.7
Kuwait	1.4	1.7	2.5	3.00	77.5	2.4	9.00	11.00	80.8
Lebanon	1.4	8.6 (2000)	4	1.20	72.5	2.3	27.00	30.00	21.5
Libya	2.3	N/A	5.9	2.00	74.4	3.2 (2000)	18.00	19.00	41.7
Oman	0.96	N/A	2.6	1.30	74.8	3.4	10.00	12.00	19.9 (2000)
Qatar	0.47	3.9 (2000)	0.81	4.50	74.1	2.9	18.00	21.00	42.5
Saudi Arabia	7.5	4.6 (2000)	23.1	2.60	72.6	3.8	21.00	26.00	309.8
Syria	7.6	12.3	19	2.50	73.8	3.2	13.50	14.50	28.4
UAE	2.7	2.3 (2000)	4.5	4.80	79.2	2.4	7.80	8.50	129.7
Yemen	5.9	11.5 (2000)	21.0	3.10	61.7	5.9	76.00	102.00	16.7
Sudan	10.5	N/A	36.2	2.00	56.7	4.1	62.00	90.00	27.9
Somalia	3.5	N/A	8.2	3.30	47.7	6.2	133.00	225.00	N/A
Algeria	13.4	20.1	32.9	1.50	71.7	2.4	34.00	39.00	101.8
Morocco	11.1	11.2	30.2	1.00	70.4	2.4	36.00	40.00	51.6
Muritania	1.2	N/A	3.1	2.90	53.7	5.6	78.00	125.00	1.8
Tunisia	3.8	14.7	10	1	73.5	2	20	24	28.7
Djibouti	0.31	N/A	0.79	1.80	53.4	4.7	88.00	133.00	0.7088
SELECTED COUNTRIES									
USA	155.5	5.5	296.4	1	77.7	2.1	6	7	12400
Sweden	4.7	6.5	9	0.4	80.5	1.8	3	4	357.7
Norway	2.5	4.4	4.6	0.7	80	1.8	3	4	295.5
Austria	4	4.9	8.2	0.7	79.4	1.4	4	5	306.1
Denmark	2.8	5.2	5.4	0.3	77.8	1.8	4	5	258.7
Finland	2.7	8.9	5.2	0.3	78.8	1.8	3	4	193.2
Singapore	2.2	5.4	4.3	N/A	N/A	N/A	N/A	N/A	N/A
Korea	24.4	3.5	48.3	0.4	77.6	1.1	5	5	791.4

Country	Exports of Goods & Services (% of GDP)	Imports of Goods & Services (% of GDP)	Foreign Direct Investment (Current US $)	Workers Remittances Received (US $)
ARAB COUNTRIES				
Bahrain	N/A	N/A	N/A	N/A
Egypt	30.3	32.6	5.4	5
Iraq	N/A	N/A	N/A	N/A
Jordan	51.9	93.4	1.5	2.5
Kuwait	67.7	30.4	0.25	N/A
Lebanon	19.7	45.1	2.6	4.9
Libya	35.0 (2000)	15.2 (2000)	N/A	0.015
Oman	59.2	31.4	0.7152	0.039
Qatar	68.3	33.5	N/A	N/A
Saudi Arabia	60.7	26.4	N/A	N/A
Syria	35.4	28.6 (2000)	0.427	0.823
UAE	94.3	76.3	N/A	N/A
Yemen	42.3	36.6	N/A	1.3
Sudan	17.8	27.6	2.3	1

Somalia	N/A	N/A	0.024	N/A
Algeria	47.8	23.6	1.1	2
Morocco	36.4	44.3	1.6	4.6
Muritania	35.9	95.7	0.115	0.002
Tunisia	48	50.6	0.723	1.4
Djibouti	36.5	53.5	0.0226	N/A
SELECTED COUNTRIES				
USA	11.2 (2000)	15.1 (2000)	109.8	2.9
Sweden	48.6	40.9	10.7	0.63
Norway	45.3	28.1	3.3	0.506
Austria	53.2	47.8	9.1	2.9
Denmark	48.6	43.9	5.2	0.868
Finland	38.7	35.2	4	0.695
Singapore	N/A	N/A	N/A	N/A
Korea	42.3	39.9	4.3	0.847
China	37.3	31.7	79.1	22.5
Japan	11.0 (2000)	9.6 (2000)	3.2	1.1
Germany	40	35.1	32	6.4

Education Indicators, Table 4
Comparing the data of the Arab countries with selected industrial countries

---

- School enrollment, primary : High

- School enrollment, secondary : Low

- School enrollment, tertiary : Low

- Ratio of girls to boys in : Some countries less than average
  primary and secondary

- Adult literacy rate (age fifteen : Low
  plus)

- Total spending on education : Less than average (except the
  GCC countries, where it is
  average).

Country	School Enrollment Primary (% Gross)	School Enrollment Secondary (% Gross)	School Enrollment Tertiary (% Gross)	Ratio of Girls to Boys in Primary & Secondary Education
ARAB COUNTRIES				
Bahrain	N/A	N/A	N/A	N/A
Egypt	100.8	85.5	33.9	93.10
Iraq	98.5	44.7	15.4	77.60
Jordan	95.8	87.3	39.2	101.20
Kuwait	97.9	94.9	19.5	102.40
Lebanon	106.3	89.1	50.7	102.20
Libya	107.3	98.4	47.8 (2000)	108.00
Oman	84.5	87.1	18.4	97.90
Qatar	106	100	18.6	98.40
Saudi Arabia	90.7	87.6	28.4	98.40
Syria	124.2	67.6	N/A	94.40
UAE	83.3	63.8	19.0 (2000)	101.70
Yemen	88.6	46.8	9.4	65.70
Sudan	60.4	34.2	N/A	89.00
Somalia	N/A	N/A	N/A	N/A
Algeria	111.8	83.1	20.3	99.20
Morocco	105.1	49.7	1.3	87.90
Muritania	93.3	20.5	3.2	97.70
Tunisia	109.4	83.9	30.2	103.1
Djibouti	40.1	23.9	2.3	75.60
SELECTED COUNTRIES				
USA	99	94.7	82.7	100.3
Sweden	96.7	102.9	81.7	100.2
Norway	98.1	113.9	79.7	100.4
Austria	106.2	102.4	50.3	96.7
Denmark	98.5	124.3	80.5	101.8
Finland	99.4	110.7	91.7	102.1
Singapore	N/A	N/A	N/A	N/A
Korea	104.8	92.9	89.9	99.9
China	112.8	74.3	20.3	99.4
Japan	100.1	101.5	55.3	100.2
Germany	101	100.2	N/A	98.7

Education Indicators (2005), Table 4

Country	Adult Literacy Rate (%) (age 15+)	Total Spending on Education as % of GDP	Ratio of Pupils to Teachers (Primary)	Ratio of Pupils to Teachers (Secondary)
ARAB COUNTRIES				
Bahrain	86.5 (2000)	3.6 (1995)	16.4	12.40
Egypt	71.4	4.7 (1995)	25.6	16.60
Iraq	74.1 (2000)	5.1 (1990)	20.5	18.80
Jordan	91.1	4.9 (2000)	20.1	18.80
Kuwait	93.3	5.1	12.1	10.30
Lebanon	N/A	2.6	14.3	8.80
Libya	84.2	2.7 (2000)	4.8	4.80
Oman	N/A	3.6	16.4	16.20
Qatar	89.0	1.6	11.1	11.60
Saudi Arabia	82.9	6.8	13.3 (1995)	12.5 (1990)
Syria	80.8	3.2 (1995)	25.3	18.10
UAE	88.7	1.3	15.2	13.10
Yemen	54.1	9.9 (2000)	22.4 (2000)	21.5 (2000)
Sudan	60.9 (2000)	12.9 (1995)	29.00	21.50
Somalia	N/A	0.4 (1985)	19.0 (1985)	N/A
SELECTED COUNTRIES				
USA	N/A	5.9	14.1	14.9
Sweden	N/A	7.4	10.1	9.7
Norway	N/A	7.7	10.5	8.8
Austria	N/A	5.5	12.4	11
Denmark	N/A	8.5	10.1 (2000)	9.6 (2000)
Finland	N/A	6.5	15.5	12.4
Singapore	92.5 (2000)	3.1 (1995)	25.3 (1995)	19.2 (2000)
Korea	N/A	4.6	29	17.8
China	90.9 (2000)	1.9 (2000)	18.6	18.3
Japan	N/A	3.6	18.9	12.6

Business Environment Indicators, Table 5
Comparing the data of the Arab countries with selected industrial countries

- Ease of doing business : Low ranking

- Starting a business : Long time

- Procedures to start a business : High

- Micro, small, and medium-size businesses : Low presence

<u>Business Environment Indicators (2005), Table 5</u>

Country	Ease of Doing Business (Economy Ranking 1-175, 1= Best)	Starting a Business (Time Required Days)	Procedures to Start a Business (Number)	Micro, small & medium size Businesses (per 1000 people)
ARAB COUNTRIES				
Bahrain	N/A	N/A	N/A	N/A
Egypt	165	19	10	25.5 (2000)
Iraq	145	77	11	N/A
Jordan	78	18	11	26.40
Kuwait	46	35	13	N/A
Lebanon	86	46	6	N/A
Libya	N/A	N/A	N/A	N/A
Oman	55	34	9	2.90
Qatar	N/A	N/A	N/A	N/A
Saudi Arabia	38	39	13	N/A
Syria	130	43	12	N/A
United Arab Emirates	77	63	12	N/A
Yemen	98	63	12.0	16.2 (2000)
Sudan	154	39	10	0.7 (2000)
Somalia	N/A	N/A	N/A	N/A
Algeria	116	24	14	18.8 (2000)
Morocco	115	12	6	15.8 (2000)
Muritania	148	82	11	N/A
Tunisia	80	11	10	0.9 (2000)
Djibouti	161	37	11	N/A
SELECTED COUNTRIES				
USA	3	5	5	20
Sweden	13	16	3	99.6

Norway	9	13	4	68.4
Austria	30	29	9	30.9
Denmark	7	5	3	47.8
Finland	14	14	3	42.4
Singapore	10	19	4	24.3
Korea	1	6	6	32.2
China	23	22	12	62.4
Japan	93	35	13	6.3 (2000)
Germany	134	35	11	0.3 (2000)

Technology Indicators, Table 6
Comparing the data of the Arab countries with selected industrial countries

- Telephone main lines per 1000 people   : Low

- Mobile subscribers per 1000 people   : Low. (except the GCC countries, where t is high)

- Internet users per 1000 people   : Low

- Personal computers per 1000 people   : Low

- Price basket for fixed line   : Low

- Price basket for mobile   : Average

- Price basket for internet   : Average

- Total telecom (revenues as percent of GDP)   : High

- Secure Internet servers   : Low

- Schools connected to the Internet   : Low

Country	Telephone main Lines (per 1000 people)	Mobile Subscribers (per 1000 people)	Internet Users (per 1000 people)	Personel Computers (per 1000 people)
ARAB COUNTRIES				
Bahrain	270	1030	213	169.00
Egypt	140	184	68	38.00
Iraq	N/A	N/A	N/A	N/A
Jordan	119	304	118	56.00
Kuwait	201	939	276	237.00
Lebanon	277	277	196	114.00
Libya	133	41	36	24.00
Oman	103	519	111	47.00
Qatar	253	882	296	171.00
Saudi Arabia	164	575	70	376.00
Syria	152	155	58	42.00
UAE	273	1000	308	197.00
Yemen	39	95	9.0	15.00
Sudan	18	50	77	90.00
Somalia	12	61	11	6.00
Algeria	78	416	58	11.00
Morocco	44	411	152	25.00
Muritania	13	253	7	14.00
Tunisia	125	566	95	57
Djibouti	14	56	13	24
SELECTED COUNTRIES				
USA	606	680	630	762
Sweden	717	935	764	763
Norway	460	1028	735	573
Austria	450	991	486	607
Denmark	619	1010	527	656
Finland	404	997	534	481
Singapore	425	1010	571	621
Korea	N/A	N/A	N/A	N/A
China	269	302	85	41
Japan	460	742	668	542
Germany	667	960	455	545

Country	Household with Television (%)	Telephone Faults (per 100 main line per year)	Price Basket for Fixed Line (US$ per month)
ARAB COUNTRIES			
Bahrain	95.0	15 (2000)	7.30
Egypt	89.0	0.1	4.00
Iraq	N/A	N/A	N/A
Jordan	96.0	10	10.00
Kuwait	95.0	4	10.50
Lebanon	93.0	N/A	15.00
Libya	N/A	N/A	N/A
Oman	79.0	89.7	12.10
Qatar	90.0	15.8	10.10
Saudi Arabia	99.0	1.7	11.70
Syria	80.0	50	2.70
UAE	86.0	0.3	17.40
Yemen	43.0	N/A	2.80
Sudan	49.0	N/A	6.30
Somalia	8.0	N/A	N/A
Algeria	88.0	0.8	6.30
Morocco	76.0	25	23.00
Muritania	21.0	N/A	11.60
Tunisia	92	30	3.7
Djibouti	41	136	16.8
SELECTED COUNTRIES			
USA	98	13.2	25
Sweden	94	N/A	26.7
Norway	100	N/A	37.9
Austria	95	5	29
Denmark	97	9	30.7
Finland	94	N/A	28.7
Singapore	99	0.3	6.7
Korea	N/A	N/A	N/A
China	89	N/A	4.7
Japan	99	N/A	26.1
Germany	95	N/A	26.5

Environment Indicators, Table 7
Comparing the data of the Arab countries with selected industrial countries

- Agricultural land (percentage) : Low

- CO2 emissions : Low (except the GCC countries, where it is high)

- Improved water source : Less than average (except the GCC countries, where it is high)

- Improved sanitation facilities : Less than average (except the GCC countries, where it is high)

- Energy use per capital : Low (except the GCC countries, where it is high)

- Electric power consumption per capita : Low (except the GCC countries, where it is high)

Country	Surface Area (Sq . Km)	Forest Area (Sq. Km)	Agricultural Land (% of Land Area)	CO2 Emission (Metric tons per Capita)
ARAB COUNTRIES				
Bahrain	N/A	N/A	N/A	N/A
Egypt	1	670	3.5	2.1 (2000)
Iraq	0.4383	8220	22.4 (2000)	2.9 (2000)
Jordan	0.08878	830	11.5 (2000)	3.2 (2000)
Kuwait	0.01782	60	8.6	32.2 (2000)
Lebanon	0.0104	1360	34.0 (2000)	4.10
Libya	1.8	2170	8.8 (2000)	8.80
Oman	0.3095	20	3.5 (2000)	9.0 (2000)
Qatar	0.011	N/A	6.5	60.0 (2000)
Saudi Arabia	2	27280	N/A	13.2 (2000)
Syria	0.1852	4610	76.2	2.9 (2000)
UAE	0.0836	3120	6.6 (2000)	35.6 (2000)
Yemen	0.528	5490	33.6 (2000)	0.80
Sudan	2.5	675500	56.3 (2000)	0.2 (2000)
Somalia	0.6377	71310	70.2 (2000)	N/A
Algeria	2.4	22770	16.8 (2000)	5.4 (2000)

Morocco	0.4466	43640	68.7 (2000)	1.20
Muritania	1	2670	38.8	0.90
Tunisia	0.1636	10560	61.5 (2000)	2.1 (2000)
Djibouti	0.0232	60	69.1 (2000)	0.5
SELECTED COUNTRIES				
USA	9.6	3	45.3	2015 (2000)
Sweden	0.4503	275300	7.8	5.2 (2000)
Norway	0.3238	93870	3.4	7.4 (2000)
Austria	0.08387	38620	39.6	7.6 (2000)
Denmark	0.04309	5000	61	8.7 (2000)
Finland	0.3382	225000	7.4	10 (2000)
Singapore	N/A	N/A	N/A	N/A
Korea	0.09926	62650	19.2	9.1 (2000)
China	9.6	2	58.8 (2000)	2.2
Japan	0.3779	248700	12.9	9.5
Germany	0.357	110800	48.8	9.7 (2000)

Privatization Process, Table 8
Comparing the data of the Arab countries with selected industrial countries

- Number of transactions and   : Relatively low (slow movement) proceeds

Country	2004		2005	
	Number of Transactions	Proceeds (Billion $)	Number of Transactions	Proceeds (Billion $)
Algeria	1	421	2	223
Djibouti	N/A	N/A	N/A	N/A
Egypt	1	52	9	2171
Iran	N/A	N/A	1	350
Jordan	1	2	1	55
Lebanon	N/A	N/A	1	236
Morocco	2	2616	1	147
Oman	N/A	N/A	2	852
Qatar	N/A	N/A	N/A	N/A
Saudi Arabia	N/A	N/A	N/A	N/A
Tunisia	1	247	3	121
Total	6	3338	20	4155

Region	Number of Transactions	Proceeds (Billion $)	Number of Transactions	Proceeds (Billion $)
East Asia & Pacific	26	7903	25	14370
Europe & Central Asia	87	14800	112	32886
Latin America & Caribbean	17	2189	9	922
Middle East & North Aftica	6	3338	20	4155
OECD	N/A	N/A	N/A	N/A
South Asia	21	4739	14	3722
Sub-Sahara Africa	9	156	13	818

Military Expenditures Indicators, Table 9
Comparing the data of the Arab countries with selected industrial countries

- Total military expenditures = 49.647 billion U.S. dollars in the Arab countries in year 2005

Countries	GDP (Billion US$)	Military Expenditures (% OF GDP)	Military Expenditures (Billion US$)	Population (Million)
Bahrain	N/A	N/A	N/A	N/A
Egypt	8937	2.8	2.51	74.00
Iraq	25.9 (2000)	N/A	N/A	24.4 (2000)
Jordan	12.7	7.7	0.97	5.50
Kuwait	80.8	5.7	4.6	2.50
Lebanon	21.5	5.2 (2004)	1.11	4.00
Libya	41.7	3.1 (2004)	1.29	5.90
Oman	19.9 (2000)	10.6	2.1	2.60
Qatar	42.5	N/A	N/A	0.81
Saudi Arabia	309.8	8.2	25.4	23.10
Syria	28.4	5.4	1.53	19.00
UAE	129.7	1.9	2.46	4.50
Yemen	16.7	5	0.83	21.00
Sudan	27.9	4.7 (2000)	1.31	36.20
Somalia	N/A	N/A	N/A	8.20
Algeria	101.8	2.8	2.85	32.90
Morocco	51.6	4.3	2.21	30.20

Muritania	1.8	1	0.018	3.10
Tunisia	28.7	1.5	0.43	10.00
Djibouti	0.7088	4.1 (2004)	0.029	0.79
SELECTED COUNTRIES				
USA	12400	4.1	508.4	296.4
Sweden	357.7	1.6	5.72	9
Norway	295.5	1.6	4.72	4.6
Austria	306.1	0.7	2.14	8.2
Denmark	258.7	1.4	3.62	5.4
Finland	193.2	1.2	2.31	5.2
Singapore	N/A	N/A	N/A	4.3
Korea	791.4	2.6	20.57	48.3
China	2200	2	44	1304.5
Japan	4500	1	45	127.8
Germany	2800	1.4	39.2	82.5

Financial Indicators, Table 10
Comparing the data of the Arab countries with selected industrial countries

Banking Sector

- Private credit to GDP : Low
- Financial system deposits to GDP : Low
- Capital adequacy ratio : High
- Non-performing loans ratio : High
- Lending-deposit rates spread : High
- Equity Market
- Number of listed firms : Few and limited
- Trade volume to GDP ratio (%) : Low (except the GCC countries, where it is high)

Banking Sector Financial Indicators, Table 10a

Country	Banking Sector -Size Index	M2 to GDP	PrivateCredit to GDP	Financial System Deposits to GDP	Banking Sector - Stability Index	Market to Book Value of Equity Ratio Median (Corporate Sector)
Bahrain	5.100	65.740	59.690	68.490	N/A	N/A
Egypt	4.460	92.360	55.650	90.520	4.290	N/A
Iraq	N/A	N/A	N/A	N/A	N/A	N/A
Jordan	6.460	123.260	75.570	103.600	4.2 (2003)	N/A
Kuwait	6.040	52.310	56.250	49.960	4.600	N/A
Lebanon	N/A	N/A	N/A	N/A	N/A	N/A
Libya	3.48 (2002)	39.750	20.700	26.670	N/A	N/A
Oman	5.394	27.460	29.190	24.460	N/A	N/A
Qatar	5.319 (2003)	47.120	29.330	44.330	N/A	N/A
Saudi Arabia	6.290	44.380	49.350	39.040	N/A	N/A
Syria	3.62 (2002)	73.050	7.800	48.260	N/A	N/A
UAE	N/A	N/A	N/A	N/A	N/A	N/A
Yemen	N/A	N/A	N/A	N/A	N/A	N/A
Sudan	N/A	N/A	N/A	N/A	N/A	N/A
Somalia	N/A	N/A	N/A	N/A	N/A	N/A
Algeria	4.420	51.000	10.280	36.200	N/A	N/A
Morocco	6.282	97.230	57.800	78.350	4.370	N/A
Muritania	N/A	N/A	N/A	N/A	N/A	N/A
Tunisia	6.240	57.040	63.300	48.650	3.240	N/A
Djibouti	N/A	N/A	N/A	N/A	N/A	N/A
USA	8.395	72.358	184.850	66.730	5.750	3.030
Sweden	6.751	48.260	106.240	89.110	5.340	2.620
Norway	7.580	55.44 (2003)	100.74 (2005)	49.960	4.460	2.450
Austria	6.860	N/A	107.120	83.490	5.090	2.000
Denmark	7.530	57.250	160.740	54.280	4.880	2.190
Finland	5.980	N/A	70.360	48.290	6.050	2.430
Singapore	7.420	109.540	109.020	105.370	5.274	1.110
Korea	7.800	69.780	125.700	77.390	4.140	1.330
China	8.190	153.550	111.780	146.780	4.160	1.590
Japan	7.010	137.800	97.940	123.120	5.490	1.830
Germany	7.090	N/A	111.030	97.920	5.120	2.020
China	9.6	2	58.8 (2000)	2.2	76 (2000)	68
Japan	0.3779	248700	12.9	9.5	100	100
Germany	0.357	110800	48.8	9.7 (2000)	100	100

Country	Capital Adequacy Ratio	Interest Coverage Ratio Median (Corporate Sector)	Liquid Assets to Total Assets	Market to Book Value of Equity Ratio Mean (Banks)	Non - performing Loans Ratio	Banking Sector - Efficiency Index
Bahrain	N/A	N/A	10.380	N/A	N/A	4.830
Egypt	14.500	N/A	24.550	N/A	25.000	5.370
Iraq	N/A	N/A	N/A	N/A	N/A	N/A
Jordan	15.9 (2003)	N/A	11.520	N/A	19.9 (2003)	4.180
Kuwait	17.300	N/A	8.980	N/A	4.500	5.570
Lebanon	23.100	N/A	67.200	N/A	15.800	4.560
Libya	N/A	N/A	7.06 (2004)	N/A	N/A	5.92 (2004)
Oman	N/A	N/A	3.741	N/A	N/A	5.275
Qatar	N/A	N/A	10.59 (2005)	N/A	N/A	N/A

Saudi Arabia	17.100	N/A	6.420	N/A	3.1 (2004)	6.124
Syria	N/A	N/A	N/A	N/A	N/A	5.711 (2005)
UAE	17.400	N/A	2.526	N/A	8.300	6.843 (2005)
Yemen	N/A	N/A	72.072	N/A	N/A	5.211 (2005)
Sudan	N/A	N/A	37.22 (2003)	N/A	N/A	4.94 (2003)
Somalia	N/A	N/A	N/A	N/A	N/A	N/A
Algeria	N/A	N/A	29.75 (2004)	N/A	N/A	5.171 (2004)
Morocco	11.500	N/A	21.740	N/A	15.700	5.215 (2004)
Muritania	N/A	N/A	N/A	N/A	N/A	3.102 (2005)
Tunisia	10.700	N/A	10.142	N/A	20.900	5.319
Djibouti	N/A	N/A	N/A	N/A	N/A	4.42 (2001)
USA	13.000	8.110	16.024	1.786	0.700	7.589
Sweden	9.900	9.070	7.643	1.828	1.100	4.743
Norway	11.900	7.270	4.030	0.650	0.700	4.726
Austria	14.500	5.550	12.500	1.290	2.2 (2003)	5.910
Denmark	13.200	7.510	5.070	1.700	N/A	4.440
Finland	17.300	10.700	14.210	2.150	0.300	4.550
Singapore	15.800	7.680	8.834	1.628	3.800	4.590
Korea	12.800	5.180	8.720	0.990	1.200	6.210
China	N/A	3.215	12.200	2.357	10.500	5.480
Japan	11.6 (2004)	19.700	8.070	1.050	1.800	6.800
Germany	13.400	5.400	19.320	1.190	4.800	6.600

Country	Three-Bank Concentration Ratios (Assets)	Three-Bank Concentration Ratios (Deposits)	Lending - Deposits Rates Spread	Net Interest Margin	Operating Costs to Total Assets	Return on Assets (Adjusted)
Bahrain	0.815	0.820	4.610	0.013	0.010	-0.023
Egypt	0.610	0.620	5.510	0.013	0.016	-0.670
Iraq	N/A	N/A	N/A	0.023 (2001)	0.005 (2001)	N/A
Jordan	0.860	0.873	4.560	0.023	0.020	-0.220
Kuwait	0.650	0.660	3.890	0.032	0.011	0.600
Lebanon	0.827	0.826	2.300	0.017	0.015	-0.510
Libya	0.849 (2002)	0.881	3.92 (2004)	0.007	0.010	-0.756
Oman	0.79 (2001)	0.787 (2001)	3.580	0.039	0.023	0.041
Qatar	N/A	N/A	N/A	0.025 (2005)	0.014	0.858
Saudi Arabia	0.567	0.562	N/A	0.032	0.015	0.827
Syria	N/A	N/A	6.930	0.015	0.006	-0.440
UAE	0.475	0.488	4.29 (2001)	0.023	0.012	0.816
Yemen	.673 (2003)	0.679	4.425 (2005)	0.039	0.020	-0.117
Sudan	0.660	0.580	N/A	.038 (2005)	0.048	-0.139
Somalia	N/A	N/A	N/A	N/A	N/A	N/A
Algeria	.795 (2002)	.864 (2002)	6.143	0.033 (2004)	.016 (2004)	-0.652
Morocco	0.572	0.565	7.620	0.023	0.024	-0.414
Muritania	N/A	N/A	13.966	0.071	0.063	0.586
Tunisia	0.580	0.560	N/A	0.024	0.027	-0.556
Djibouti	N/A	N/A	10.210	.022 (2003)	.034 (2003)	N/A
USA	0.139	0.146	2.587	0.026	0.031	-0.157
Sweden	0.790	0.840	2.505	0.010	0.011	-0.541
Norway	0.780	0.826	2.170	0.015	0.013	-0.521
Austria	0.480	0.560	N/A	0.015	0.017	-0.670
Denmark	0.820	0.800	4.5 (2002)	0.013	0.010	-0.500
Finland	0.800	0.840	N/A	0.011	0.016	-0.060
Singapore	0.824	0.822	4.838	0.016	0.011	-0.357
Korea	0.455	0.452	1.800	0.027	0.015	-0.560
China	0.600	0.620	3.250	0.019	0.011	-0.723
Japan	0.359	0.353	1.400	0.011	0.012	-1.010
Germany	0.390	0.420	N/A	0.010	0.013	-0.930

Equity Market Indicators (2005), Table 10b

Country	Equity Market Index	Equity Market- Size Index	Number of Listed Firms	Market Capitalization to GDP ratio (%)	New Capital Raised to Market Capitalization (%)
Bahrain	N/A	N/A	47.00	119.60	N/A
Egypt	5.10	5.40	744.00	66.30	2.00
Iraq	N/A	N/A	N/A	N/A	N/A
Jordan	N/A	5.25 (2002)	201 (2005)	218.50	1.28 (2002)
Kuwait	N/A	N/A	143.00	134.10	1.13 (2002)
Lebanon	N/A	5.15	11.00	16.30	42.90
Libya	N/A	N/A	N/A	N/A	N/A
Oman	N/A	N/A	96.00	23.1 (2003)	8.50
Qatar	N/A	N/A	31.00	N/A	N/A
Saudi Arabia	N/A	9.71	77.00	154.20	0.24
Syria	N/A	N/A	N/A	N/A	N/A
United Arab Emirates	N/A	N/A	79.00	N/A	0.58
Yemen	N/A	N/A	N/A	N/A	N/A
Sudan	N/A	N/A	N/A	N/A	N/A
Somalia	N/A	N/A	N/A	N/A	N/A
Algeria	N/A	N/A	N/A	N/A	N/A
Morocco	4.45 (2004)	5.1 (2004)	56.00	50.90	5.6 (2004)
Muritania	N/A	N/A	40 (2001)	113.3 (2001)	N/A
Tunisia	N/A	5.1 (2002)	46.00	9.70	0.37 (2002)
Djibouti	N/A	N/A	N/A	N/A	N/A
USA	6.60	7.50	5145.00	134.90	0.70
Sweden	6.20	7.04	303.00	111.10	0.90
Norway	5.00	6.30	191.00	58.90	3.08
Austria	4.95	5.20	92.00	35.00	3.16
Denmark	5.50	6.00	186.00	65.20	0.76
Finland	5.50	7.20	153.00	102.60	1.90
Singapore	5.80	6.80	564.00	163.90	2.03
Korea	6.25	7.60	1620.00	73.10	2.90
China	5.10	6.50	1387.00	35.30	3.80
Japan	7.23	9.05	3386.00	106.00	1.02
Germany	5.70	6.30	648.00	43.80	2.10

Country	Trade Volume to GDP ratio (%)	Equity Market - Stability Index	Equity return Volatility (%)	Probability of Earnings Manipulation (%)	Equity Market Efficiency Index
Bahrain	5.40	5.5 (2004)	21.03	N/A	N/A
Egypt	28.40	5.80	11.60	N/A	4.08
Iraq	N/A	N/A	N/A	N/A	N/A
Jordan	185.10	4.10	23.70	N/A	N/A
Kuwait	125.90	12.15	21.55	N/A	N/A
Lebanon	4.10	11.99	25.30	N/A	N/A
Libya	N/A	N/A	N/A	N/A	N/A
Oman	5.7 (2003)	6.90	14.07	N/A	N/A
Qatar	N/A	N/A	N/A	N/A	N/A

Saudi Arabia	356.20	4.938 (2004)	18.96	N/A	N/A
Syria	N/A	N/A	N/A	N/A	N/A
United Arab Emirates	N/A	N/A	N/A	N/A	N/A
Yemen	N/A	N/A	N/A	N/A	N/A
Sudan	N/A	N/A	N/A	N/A	N/A
Somalia	N/A	N/A	N/A	N/A	N/A
Algeria	N/A	N/A	N/A	N/A	N/A
Morocco	8.01	4.20	16.38	N/A	3.80
Muritania	N/A	N/A	N/A	N/A	N/A
Tunisia	1.58	4.60	13.60	N/A	N/A
Djibouti	N/A	N/A	N/A	N/A	N/A
USA	172.70	5.40	11.90	6.10	6.90
Sweden	131.00	5.20	14.50	16.60	6.50
Norway	68.60	4.70	16.40	19.20	4.00
Austria	15.00	4.90	13.30	10.50	4.60
Denmark	59.70	5.17	12.20	16.90	5.20
Finland	141.50	4.40	20.10	12.30	4.90
Singapore	102.60	5.30	13.33	29.20	5.40
Korea	152.70	4.40	21.80	22.20	6.60
China	26.30	4.80	17.70	22.50	3.90
Japan	110.90	4.99	16.19	8.60	7.66
Germany	63.30	4.50	19.80	14.60	6.20

Country	Market Capitalization Concentration in Top 10 Firms (%)	Percentage of Private Information Trading	Transaction Cost %	Percentage of Zero Return Weeks
Bahrain	94.50	N/A	N/A	45.19 (2004)
Egypt	48.80	7.60	N/A	11.18
Iraq	N/A	N/A	N/A	N/A
Jordan	85.60	N/A	N/A	5.7 (2004)
Kuwait	N/A	N/A	N/A	42.3 (2004)
Lebanon	73.3 (2004)	N/A	N/A	N/A
Libya	N/A	N/A	N/A	N/A
Oman	73.10	N/A	N/A	11.5 (2004)
Qatar	N/A	N/A	N/A	N/A
Saudi Arabia	79.82	N/A	N/A	5.76 (2004)
Syria	N/A	N/A	N/A	N/A
United Arab Emirates	N/A	N/A	N/A	N/A
Yemen	N/A	N/A	N/A	N/A
Sudan	N/A	N/A	N/A	N/A
Somalia	N/A	N/A	N/A	N/A
Algeria	N/A	N/A	N/A	N/A
Morocco	94.80	4.00	5.4 (2004)	13.46
Muritania	N/A	N/A	N/A	N/A
Tunisia	62.80	N/A	N/A	25 (2004)
Djibouti	N/A	N/A	N/A	N/A

Djibouti	N/A	N/A	N/A	N/A
USA	12.10	5.10	1.20	36.90
Sweden	61.00	4.20	4.06	3.12
Norway	71.90	5.20	3.80	5.90
Austria	86.30	8.50	3.40	14.72
Denmark	75.00	11.40	3.30	6.80
Finland	85.40	4.70	2.50	4.25
Singapore	60.80	2.30	5.13	11.36
Korea	44.30	8.40	3.20	0.60
China	28.30	3.30	1.17	7.96
Japan	23.80	6.00	3.20	1.73
Germany	63.20	3.77	5.30	8.60

Enterprise Surveys, Table 11
Comparing the data of the Arab countries with selected industrial countries

- Corruption indicators : High value
- Bureaucracy indicators : High value
- Courts : High value
- Crime indicators : Low value
- Informality indicators : Low value
- Infrastructure indicators : High value

COUNTRY OR REGION	Unofficial Payments for Typical Firms to get things done (% of sales)(lower value is better)	Senior Management Time Spend In Dealing With Requirements of Government Regulations (%)(Lower value is better)	Time Spent Resolving a Dispute (Weeks)(Lower value is better)	Losses Due To Theft, Robbery, Vandalism & Arson against the Firm (% of sales)(Lower value is better)	Sales Amount Reported By a Typical Firm for Tax purposes (%)(Higher Value is better)
East Asia & Pacific	1.7	6.95	69.83	0.79	73.37
Europe & Central Asia	1.04	5.4	55.18	0.4	86.8
Latin America	1.4	11.14	55.01	1.51	76.63
Middle East (MENA)	1.87	8.44	66.63	0.28	77.4
OECD	0.13	2.97	73.6	0.21	93.55
South Asia	2.02	7.1	53.72	0.47	83.39
Sub-Sahara Africa	2.14	7.96	60.42	2.06	70.29
ARAB COUNTRIES					
Algeria (2002)	6.04	N/A	72.74	0.51	72.5
Egypt (2004)	1.34	N/A	N/A	N/A	83.2
Jordan (2006)	0.11	6.67	N/A	0.08	88.4
Lebanon (2006)	2.48	11.97	30.23	N/A	65.6
Mauritania	3.77	5.84	N/A	5.56	52.4
Morocco (2004)	N/A	7.55	76.48	0.05	97.8
Oman (2003)	1.01	N/A	87.08	N/A	71.1
Syria (2003)	N/A	10.31	N/A	N/A	51.1

Enterprise Surveys: Corruption Indicators (2006), Table 11

COUNTRY OR REGION	Delay in Obtaining an Electrical Connection (Days)(Lower value is better)	Number of Electrical Outages (Days)(Lower value is better)	Value Lost Due to Electrical Outages (% of sales)(Lower value is better)	Number of Water supply failures (Days)(Lower value is better)	Delay in Obtaining a mainline telephone connection days(Lower value is better)
East Asia & Pacific	19.37	9.3	2.54	3.52	15.76
Europe & Central Asia	9.31	14.03	3.14	7.54	13.35
Latin America & Caribbean	32.88	17.78	3.55	14.48	45.06
Middle East & North Africa	53.68	46.12	4.2	41.73	49.9
OECD	9.73	1.53	2.34	0.25	9.03
South Asia	56.26	121.51	5.56	12.03	66.31
Sub-Sahara Africa	43.76	56.36	5.73	37.19	58.39
ARAB COUNTRIES					
Algeria (2002)	124.94	13.99	4.27	41.78	174.99
Egypt (2004)	99.44	17.46	4.57	8.5	136.88
Jordan (2006)	47.11	N/A	1.10	N/A	3.28
Lebanon (2006)	40.29	188.58	5.97	22.11	2.42
Mauritania	7.52	44.52	1.38	92.54	14.49
Morocco (2004)	8.24	7.28	0.59	1.78	4.37
Oman (2003)	10.49	5.66	4.18	37.8	7.02
Syria (2003)	61.79	43.77	8.58	138.41	58.38

The various indicators reflected that the other face of the hate culture is corruption, ignorance, oppression, and poverty. Lack of democracy and unfair distribution of wealth in the Middle East resulted in the disintegration of the Lebanese and the Arab societies. Every person and every family were forced to seek refuge in a religious group to provide them protection. The competition and struggle between the various religious groups became more fierce and ugly. People became more selfish, especially with more poverty and less medical and social benefits. Loyalty to the country is replaced with loyalty to the religious groups. Increasing numbers of families sought hope in the American dream. Large number of families and young entrepreneurs immigrated to the USA and countries worldwide. The political and social oppression in the Middle East forced millions of the best minds and well educated, highly motivated people out of their countries. I strongly believe that this brain drain is the most precious loss in the Middle East.

Chapter Three

Moment of Truth

The fragmentation of the Lebanese society reached a critical point. The various religious groups are competing against each other to get larger share of the limited economic resources of the country. With stagnant gross domestic product and growing population, the share per family of the country's wealth decreases, which reduces the quality of education and medical care. In turn the people became more desperate, angry, and vicious.

The logical thing to do is increase the productivity of the Lebanese people, which will increase the gross domestic product. In turn the families will be richer and happier. Obviously doing it requires getting the best from everyone—in other words, achieving the American dream in every village and city in Lebanon and the Middle East. So, instead of immigrating to the United States of America, we bring the USA to every house and city in the Middle East. The keyword for this process is FREEDOM. Achieving the American dream in Lebanon and the Middle East requires the following:

Kindly note that the followings items are quotes from the Declaration of Independence and the Constitution of the United States of America. I recommend having the same concepts in the Lebanese constitution.)

- Congress shall make no law respecting on establishment of religion or prohibiting the free exercise thereof, or abridging the freedom of speech, or of the press; or the right of the people peaceably to assemble, and to petition the government for a redress of grievances (Article I).

- The right of the people to be secure in their persons, houses, papers, and effects, against unreasonable searches and seizures, shall not be violated (Article IV).

- In all criminal prosecutions, the accused shall enjoy the right to a speedy and public trial, - - - - - , and to be informed of the nature and cause of the accusation; to be confronted with the witnesses against him, to have compulsory process for obtaining witnesses in his favor, and to have the assistance of counsel for his defense. (Article VI).

- Neither slavery nor involuntary servitude, except as a punishment for crime whereof the party shall have been duly convicted shall exist within the United States, or any place subject to their jurisdiction (Article XIII).

- All persons born or naturalized in the United States, and subject to the jurisdiction thereof, are citizens of the United States and of the state wherein they reside. No state shall make or enforce any law which shall abridge the privileges or immunities of citizens of the United States; nor shall any state deprive any person of life, liberty, or property, without due process of law; nor deny to any person within its jurisdiction the equal protection of the laws (Article XIV).

- The right of citizens of the United States to vote shall not be denied or abridged by the United States or by any state on account of race, color, or previous condition of servitude (Article XV).

- The right of citizens of the Untied States to vote shall not be denied or abridged by the United States or by any state on account of sex (Article XIX).

The items mentioned above ensure that every person will have an equal opportunity to get an education, medical care, and justice in all aspects of life. As indicated by the Declaration of Independence of the United States of America on July 4, 1776:

ALL men are created equal, that they are endowed by their Creator with certain unalienable rights, that among these are life, liberty, and the pursuit of happiness - - - .

Doing all of this is difficult because it requires free leaders who reject oppression and corruption. Doing it will result in getting the best of everyone, increasing the gross domestic product, and improving the living standards in Lebanon and the Middle East.

To do it, I suggest the following steps:

STEP ONE:	**The Arab leaders should accept and take the responsibility for the problems and difficulties in the Middle East. (The conspiracy theory is not true.)**
STEP TWO:	**Working hard to increase the country's productivity and wealth is better than fighting each other to get a larger piece of the limited wealth available currently.**
STEP THREE:	**Eliminate all aspects of religious discrimination in Lebanon completely.**
STEP FOUR:	**Acknowledge the importance of the time factor in the change process.**
STEP FIVE:	**The international military presence is more effective to bring peace and stability to the Middle East. The experience of the Gulf Cooperation Council (GCC) countries.**
STEP SIX:	**Promote the American dream in Lebanon.**

STEP ONE:	**The Arab leaders should accept and take the responsibility of the problems and difficulties in the Middle East. (The conspiracy theory is not true.)**

The gross domestic product of the Gulf Cooperation Council (GCC) countries in year 2005 reached $582.7 billion U.S., which represents a small percentage of the GDP of the industrial countries. The oil revenues in the Arab countries in year 2006 reached $466 billion U.S. **So it is obvious that the oil is valuable to the free world as a product. The value paid for it is not the main issue.** Please note that the money paid in Afghanistan and Iraq's war up till 2007 exceeded $3,500 billion U.S., which is more than six times the oil revenues of the Arab countries in 2005. In addition to that, more than three thousand American soldiers died and thousands more suffered from injuries. So we conclude that:

A. **Oil as a commodity and a source of energy is essential for the whole world as a product. (This is a common knowledge.)**

B. **If the political systems in the Middle East are as stable as they are in the European countries (as an example), the USA would never bother to interfere or use military force at all, because the production and flow of oil to the free countries would be secure and safe. All countries would buy oil from the world markets at market prices.**

Table 12
GDP in the Oil-Rich GCC Countries Compared to the GDP in Selected Countries in 2005

Country	GDP (U.S. $ Billion)	Population (Millions)
Bahrain		0.73
Kuwait	80.8	2.5
Oman	19.9	2.6
Qatar	42.5	0.81
Saudi Arabia	309.8	23.1
United Arab Emirates	129.7	4.5
Total GCC Countries	582.7	34.24
USA	12400	296.4
Japan	4500	127.8
Germany	2800	82.5
France	2100	60.9
United Kingdom	2200	60.2
Sweden	357.7	9.5
Austria	306.1	8.2
China	2200	1304.5
Korea	791.4	48.3

Table (13)
Oil Revenues in OPEC Countries (U.S.$ Billion)

OPEC Countries	2006	2007	2008		2006
Algeria	45	50	60	**Algeria**	45
Angola	31	44	61		
Indonesia	-3	-4	-6		
Iran	55	56	61		
Iraq	32	36	40	**Iraq**	40
Kuwait	50	54	63	**Kuwait**	63
Libya	36	40	46	**Libya**	46
Nigeria	52	55	64		
Qatar	24	27	32	**Qatar**	32
Saudi Arabia	183	190	213	**Saudi Arabia**	183
United Arab Emirates	87	62	74	**UAE**	57
Venezuela	43	48	52		
TOTAL	605	658	762	**TOTAL**	466

<u>Source</u>: *Alwatan* newspaper. Issue number 2604, November 16, 2007.

Unfortunately the Middle East area is unstable. **The hate culture in Lebanon, Iraq, and the Middle East is the main problem. The conspiracy theory is not true at all. The civil wars and the religious feud between Muslims and Christians started in Lebanon and the surrounding area hundreds of years ago.** Also, the infighting between Shia Muslims and Sunni Muslims in Iraq in the whole area started 1350 years ago and continued during the Umayyads' rule of the Muslim empire (AD 660–750) with <u>Damascus</u> as their capital and later when the sons of the Prophet Mohammad's uncle Abul Abbas defeated the Umayyad and established the Abbasids' rule of the Muslim empire (AD 750) and built the city of <u>Baghdad</u> in Iraq to be their capital.

The Abbasids asked the Persians to help them establish their rule. Later they killed some of the Persian leaders who had helped them establish their empire, such as Abu Muslim Al-Kharasani and years later the Baramkes family.

A major event during this period is well known. After the death of Sultan Haroun AlRashid, his son Alamin (from an Arab wife) replaced him as Sultan of the Muslim empire, and the other son, Almamoun (from a Persian wife), became the crown prince and took over as head of the Persian Muslim areas. Later the Almamoun (from a Persian mother) sent his armies from Persia to Baghdad to kill and behead his brother, Alamin (from an Arab mother), and replaced him as Sultan of the Muslim empire with Baghdad as the capital.

Wars, hate, bloodshed, and savage events started in Iraq and the Middle East more than 1,400 years ago, long before the discovery of America and the establishing the United States of America. The hate culture had been the real problem in the Middle East for hundreds of years. Certainly it is not the USA, even in the case of the Arab-Israel conflict in modern history. It is well-known that the various American administrations tried to find a peaceful end to this conflict. Unfortunately the Arab leaders and the media were not fair in judging the USA. Some Americans support Israel for religious reasons. Others considered Israel a good friend in the war against the communists during the Soviet Union era. Let us remember that America supported the Europeans during the second world war. They also supported the Koreans, helped the Vietnamese against the communists, and they supported the Muslims in Bosnia. **This is the main characteristic of America.**

America supports Israel to make sure that the Israelis feel safe and secure. It is very important. Unfortunately, on the Arab side, the leaders always give the public an impression that they are very close to defeating Israel, and they put the blame for not doing it on the USA. The Arab leaders and the media ignore that the Israelis have had nuclear weapons since the '60s. Obviously, if threatened seriously, they will use these weapons to defend their existence, and in such a case we will have a different map in the Middle East. **Only a naïve person would think that the Israeli people will follow the steps of the crusaders by boarding ships and leaving the Middle East. The Israelis will not keep their nuclear weapons in boxes and leave, asking the Arab leaders to dust them occasionally. They will use them to defend their existence, and a new map for the Middle East will emerge.**

Obviously the U.S. support of Israel is keeping all the Middle East countries secure and safe from real disaster. The Arab leaders and media ignore this fact and keep fueling the hate culture by giving the public the illusion that they are very close to victory, but the blame is on the U.S. and Europe. **This case of denial and not accepting the responsibility of their actions and mistakes created this ugly environment of hate and resentment toward the USA and the Christians.**

I strongly believe that this environment resulted in:

A. Preventing the normal development of the social and political systems in the Middle East.

B. Providing the extremists the opportunity to grow.

STEP TWO: **Working hard to increase the country's productivity and wealth is better than fighting each other to get a larger piece of the limited wealth available currently.**

The hate culture resulted in the various religious groups fighting each other fiercely to get a larger share of the limited wealth in the country, which led to more poverty and increasing immigration of the well-educated and highly motivated entrepreneurs.

The best approach is to increase the productivity of the whole country, which in turn increases the share of every person, family, and group. Achieving this target requires that fairness, equality, stability, and rule of law prevails in the country. Several small countries, such as Denmark, Austria, and Sweden, where the population is less than 9 million, reached a gross domestic product of $300 billion U.S. annually (ten times the productivity of the average Arab person). So empowering the people of Lebanon and the Middle East (309 million) is expected to double (at least) or triple the non-oil revenues, which means an additional revenue of more than $1,000 billion. Obviously the people in the Middle East will enjoy better living standards and happiness throughout the area. Establishing the peace culture is the key factor.

STEP THREE:	Eliminate all aspects of religious discrimination in Lebanon completely.

The common agreement by all groups in Lebanon to base political appointments on religion aimed to have equal and fair distribution of the government jobs among all religious sects. But this system resulted in continuous conflicts and civil wars.

Eliminating the religious discrimination is essential to build modern Lebanon and to stop the brain drain.

STEP FOUR:	Acknowledge the importance of the time factor in the change process.

The problems in Lebanon and the Middle East started hundreds of years ago. It will take years to solve them. Building confidence and trust among the various groups (local and regional) is expected to take time. Separating religion from the state and educating the public on peace requires:

A. Reasonable time period

B. Full commitment by the government in Lebanon, Iraq, and the Middle East

C. Full participation by schools and universities

D. Effective participation of media

E. Student exchange programs between the Middle East countries and the free world

Keep in mind that confidence-building measures are needed to get the various religious groups together again. Doing it requires educating the public, which takes years.

STEP FIVE:	The international military presence is more effective to bring peace and stability to the Middle East. The experience of the Gulf Cooperation Council (GCC) countries.

Japan forced the USA to join the second world war by attacking the U.S. Navy base in Hawaii. Millions died during the war. When it ended the USA provided Japan and Germany with billions of U.S. dollars and helped both countries rebuild their infrastructure, universities, highways, factories, airports, and seaports. Over the last sixty years, both countries became the most important economic powers next to the USA. Currently China is moving forward.

If the conspiracy theory is true, then both Japan and Germany were supposed to be poor and destroyed, like Somalia as an example. There are still American military bases in both countries now. This fact is considered to be an advantage for both countries because it provided them with protection and a safety net at a minimum cost instead of their spending billions of U.S. dollars every year on arms and weapons. The money went to build universities, schools, hospitals, and factories. The gross domestic product of Japan was $4,500 billion U.S. in 2005. The GDP of Germany reached $2,800 billion U.S.

The current status of Japan and Germany is a true and good indicator of the human and advanced nature of the American social and political system. The people and the leaders in Lebanon, Iraq, and the Middle East should learn from the Japanese and German experience. President Mubarak, in a recent speech, said that the situation in Lebanon and the Middle East is critical. Yes, it is true. Personally I believe that it means we should work harder to reach peace. Let us explore the fears of the various local and regional parties involved in Lebanon.

1. The Lebanese people are divided as usual into two main groups:

A. Several leaders. Some of them cooperated with the Syrians in the past. Currently they are interested in having a free Lebanon. This group includes Christians, Druze, and Sunni Muslims.

B. Several leaders who are afraid of Israel and do not trust the USA. This group includes Shia Muslims and few Christian and Sunni Muslim leaders. In general they are loyal to Syria and Iran.

   Both groups succeeded in having hundreds of thousands demonstrators in the streets of Beirut. So it is difficult for one group alone to take control of the situation.

2. Syria aimed always to take over Lebanon. Syria rejects exchanging ambassadors with Lebanon. It armed Hezballah (a Shia Muslim party) and also armed several extreme Palestinian groups. Syria occupied Lebanon for thirty years and always rejected disarming the Palestinian refugee camps because Syria considers it a service to Israel. Syria is afraid of Israel and considers an independent Lebanon a potential danger and an extension of Israel.

3. Israel lives in fear of persecution and is under siege always. Sometimes it views offensive measures as the best method to defend its limited geographical space. The September 11 experience supports Israeli fears.

The current sharp split in Lebanon is linked to the regional conflict. The hate culture is expected to take Lebanon to a fate similar as the Somali case. I strongly believe that the peace culture is the only hope for Lebanon. In this regard I suggest following the example of the Gulf Cooperation Council (GCC) countries (Qatar, Saudi Arabia, Bahrain, Kuwait, - - - -). Lebanon should seek direct assistance from the USA or the United Nations to send military forces to establish long-term military bases in Lebanon, to do the same functions of the military bases in the GCC countries, Japan and Germany.

The GCC countries' experience supports my position. Thousands of the American soldiers are mostly Christians; some are Jews, Muslims, and others. They came from different cities and states—California, Montana, Texas, Alabama, Florida, etc. The best kids in the USA sacrificed a lot to protect and guarantee the security and safety of the peoples of Qatar, Kuwait, Saudi Arabia, and Bahrain. Few voices here and there say that the USA did it to protect the oil fields. I say, so what. There are mutual benefits for all parties concerned. This strategic alliance between the GCC countries and the USA gave the peoples in the GCC countries the opportunity to develop their countries and live in dignity.

Tables 3 to 11 indicate that the GCC countries succeeded in achieving good results in the areas of education, medical care, infrastructure, and basic utilities such as electricity and water, etc.

This is exactly why I recommend we have the American dream in the Middle East. The dream of every human being is to have a happy, free, stable, fair, just, and safe life; to protect children and women from abuse (physical and verbal); in short, to bring the American dream and way of life to Lebanon, Iraq, and the Middle East.

Establishing American or United Nations military bases in Lebanon would protect the Lebanese people from the regional influence. It would bring peace to the hearts of a large group of the Lebanese people (group A) and Israel.

On the other hand, certain steps should be taken to satisfy the other group (B) of the Lebanese people, because they are afraid that by putting down their arms they will return to the previous situation in the past, when they were treated like second-class citizens and had only a small share of the limited economic resources of Lebanon.

To deal with their fears, I suggest the following:

- Eliminating the religious discrimination in all political and government jobs, including the top positions: the president, prime minister, the speaker of the parliament, ministers, etc..

- All groups start negotiations immediately under the supervision of the United Nations to prepare a new constitution for Lebanon, separating religion from the state.

And provide all citizens freedom and equal rights. I suggest giving them three years to finish this task.

- In case they failed to do it in three years (failed to agree on something) then the United Nations should select and form an international committee of experts to do this task in one year. (Forming the committee should be done within a six-month period.)

- The international committee of experts should finish the task within one year.

- When the committee finishes this task, elections should be conducted in Lebanon within six months.

Then the elected Lebanese government and president should start the long process of restructuring and organizing the whole country in a similar manner to what the GCC countries are doing, such as:

A. Establishing councils (Shoura) to allow the citizens to participate in the political system.

B. Conducting elections in municipalities to allow the people to participate in managing their affairs.

C. Building more schools and universities. In Saudi Arabia the government already sent more than twenty thousand young men and women to international universities in the USA, Canada, Europe, and Asia (graduate and undergraduate programs). The reader can imagine the impact of this large group of students when they return to Saudi Arabia after five years. I strongly believe that they will contribute positively to the social, economic, and political development of the country.

D. Developing the financial system (the financial markets, institutions, and securities) by giving more licenses to stock brokerage firms and insurance companies. This will increase the volume of credit facilities and funding to the private sector, especially small and medium-size companies which in turn support economic development and job creation.

E. Modifying the judicial system to ensure justice and equal rights to all.

F. Establishing new policies and procedures to fight corruption and improve the tax system in the country.

Doing all of this depends on the political stability in the country and the presence of the American military bases.

STEP SIX: Promote the American dream in Lebanon.

The Lebanese people suffered through the civil wars and the Arab-Israel conflict, especially the population in Southern Lebanon and Bekaa Valley. The majority of the population in this area is Shia Muslims. There are no five-star hotels or advanced, modern hospitals and universities in the area. The available institutions there are simple, while the other areas of Lebanon, especially the capital, Beirut, enjoy the benefits of modern institutions. A strong feeling of resentment developed within the population in this area.

In this regard I believe that group (B) of the Lebanese people consists of the following segments:

1. Several members of the leaders are linked directly with the interests and policies of Syria and Iran.

2. The average normal citizens suffered for a long time from poverty and lack of medical care, proper education, and good job opportunities. Moreover, up to the '60s a large number of the villages in this area did not have water or electricity in their houses. In some villages the people used to drink from large pools of water along with their cattle. The pro-Syrian politicians took advantage of the situation. During the Syrian occupation, they benefited from the Syrian and Iranian support and built roads, small hospitals, and schools in southern Lebanon and Bekaa valley area. Obviously this strategy worked for the pro-Syrian politicians and attracted the population in the area, especially the Shia Muslims.

To deal with this situation, Lebanon needs a large-scale effort to improve the infrastructure in this area and all over Lebanon through building a network of medical centers, schools, and universities. Also it must build a network of small roads in the villages and rural areas to help the farmers. Moreover, it must build small dams in the country to save the water and generate electricity. The water of the rivers is wasted in the sea. Saving the precious water and generating more electricity would support the Lebanese economy and enable Lebanon to share the available water with Israel, Jordan, and Syria. It would be a positive factor. Such projects and services would give the population a sense of dignity and happiness and increase their loyalty to their country. One of the projects that I suggest is building a large hospital (Christ Medical Center) in the village of Cannas, where the Christ performed several miracles by healing sick people. This village is populated by Shia Muslims. The change from the hate culture to the peace culture in Lebanon would open new horizons for the Lebanese people and provide every citizen with a real chance to achieve the American dream in Lebanon. In this regard the following steps are essential:

A. Eliminating religious discrimination in government positions. (Separate religion from the state.)

B. Establishing a strategic alliance and American military bases in Lebanon to ensure security and stability.

C. Passing state laws to prevent the parliament members from joining the government as ministers, to guarantee that the government fulfills its function as an executive system. And the parliament members must supervise and monitor the government performance. This situation means that the executive branch would be the president and his government (members with professional experience), supervised and audited by:

- The parliament
- The judicial system
- The media

So we will have one head for the country, not three, as we have now in Lebanon. And they rarely agree on anything.

D. Passing state laws to force the government members and top government employees to allow the tax department to publicize their income tax statements annually as long as they are in office.

E. Establishing policies and procedures to fight corruption and misuse of government funds.

F. Empowering the judicial system in the country and protecting the courts from any interference by the politicians.

G. Empowering the media because it is a strong, independent auditing authority.

H. Improving the educational system, especially the quality of the public sector, and connecting the schools to the Internet system.

I. Disarming the Palestinian camps. I suggest asking the United Nations to have a military presence in the camps for at least ten years to ease the tensions and fears of the Palestinians.

Also the Lebanese government should:

- Provide the Palestinians permanent residence cards to facilitate their travel in and out of Lebanon, and give people the right and the opportunity to work so that they can support themselves and their families.

- The Palestinians residing in Lebanon should have similar rights to the ones the Lebanese immigrants have in the USA, Canada, and Europe. After five years of residence in Lebanon, the Palestinians should have the right to apply for Lebanese citizenship. Also, all Palestinians born in Lebanon should have the right to get Lebanese citizenship directly.

- Provide the Palestinians the right to buy houses and land in Lebanon and the right to establish businesses and companies.

J. Developing the Lebanese financial system—the financial markets, institutions, and securities—which in turn facilitates the funding of the new business and companies in the country.

The most important element is to have a strong will to fight for a free Lebanon. Unfortunately Lebanon missed a rare opportunity in 2005. On February, 13, 2005, the evil forces assassinated the former prime minister, Rafiq Alhariri, in Beirut. More than a million Lebanese demonstrated in the streets of Beirut, demanding full withdrawal of Syria from Lebanon. The free world supported them. The prime minister resigned. The Lebanese leaders of the free movement were supposed to keep the momentum and take the following measures:

1. Demand the resignation of the Lebanese president.

2. Replace the key government officials because the members of the current team were appointed under full supervision of the Syrian officials during the Syrian occupation of Lebanon.

3. Eliminate officially all types of religious discrimination in the country, especially in the appointments of officials in government positions. Failing to do it coupled with the information spread in the country that the Christian clergy demanded that all calls for the resignation of the Christian president should be stopped. This situation pushed the Lebanese Shia Muslims back to the corner of the extreme Shia leaders.

4. Replace the hate culture in Israel with a peace treaty. The Lebanese leaders did not do it. On the contrary, they kept repeating that Israel is the

enemy for Lebanon and the Lebanese people. This attitude supported Hezballah claim that Lebanon is still at war with Israel, the enemy. So this justified them and their supporters keeping the arms and maintaining their aggressive behavior against Israel, which lead to the July 2006 war.

The Lebanese leaders' hesitation to stand up and change the hate culture and adopt the peace culture resulted in wasting a rare opportunity. It will cost the Lebanese people precious time and lots of blood and tears. You cannot go to war halfheartedly. The Lebanese leaders were supposed to be fully committed and go all the way. There is no gray area between the hate culture and the peace culture.

There is no one Lebanon. Currently there is a group of small communities representing different religious and sectarian groups. Either they go separately as fragmented, small emirates or they build a new free country together in a similar manner as the immigrants did in America. Achieving the American dream in Lebanon is the only hope.

I strongly believe that the peace culture is the way to reach a free, independent Lebanon.

CHAPTER FOUR

The American Dream in the Middle East

Hate and Blood in Iraq

The best young American men and women came to Iraq to help and save the Iraqi people and the neighboring countries from a dictator who abused the people and ruled savagely for a long period of time. Moreover, he was preparing his sons to take over later. So the whole area was on hold and threatened for years to come. Instead of thanking the American soldiers, the hate culture resulted in the death of thousands of them by the hands of the Iraqi people. Saddam Hussein used chemical weapons against the Kurds and killed thousands of Shia Muslims and Sunni Muslims during his rule. The religious discrimination in Iraq, which started hundreds of years ago and prevailed during Saddam's rule, is the major factor in Iraq today fueling the bloodshed and the civil war. The best solution is the peace culture. The German or Japanese experience is an excellent example of the future Iraq in the case of the peace culture.

Establishing long-term American military bases to protect the Iraqi people from external threats, while the Iraqi people and national army manage the internal situation, is perfect. Iraq is rich with economic resources—enough to rebuild the country within few years of peace. Any illusions of repeating Saddam's military games and hostile adventures are useless. The Kurdish leaders are rational and working seriously on building a new, modern society. They are building the basic infrastructure in Kurdistan: electricity, water, highways, airports, and hospitals, etc. The Sunni Muslims and Shia Muslims have the choice to build the peace culture and enjoy life in a free, safe, modern Iraq with religion separate from the state or in continuing the one hundred years of savage religious civil war.

The other face of the threat in Iraq is the regional factor.

The neighbors of Iraq are:

A. The Gulf Cooperation Council (GCC) countries, which include Saudi Arabia, Kuwait, Qatar, Bahrain, Oman, and the United Arab Emirates. They supported Iraq for a long period of time. Their main concern is to see Iraq stable, united, and peaceful. An aggressive or biased leadership in Iraq is a threat to everyone.

B. Turkey. Its concern is the Kurdish issue; an independent growing Kurdistan is considered a threat because it provides a good example for the Kurds in Turkey, Iran, and Syria. Moreover, in the case of a disintegrated Iraq, Turkey will be interested in the city of Karkuk and its surrounding oil-rich area.

C. Jordan. Once the Hashemite family ruled Iraq. In case of a collapse in Iraq, Jordan can help by ruling the Sunni Muslim tribes.

D. Iran and Syria. The Iranian president, Najjad, threatened Israel publicly. Obviously he did not notice the fate of the ex-president in Iraq, Saddam Hussein, who threatened Israel once.

In the past I remember that Israeli Prime Minister Menahaim Pegen once mentioned in a press conference that in case there was a real threat from Iran (the Iranians were threatening to march to Israel), the Israeli army would meet them halfway.

Please keep in mind the following:

In Iran the population is made up of mostly Shia Muslims.

In Iraq a large segment of the population made up of is Shia Muslims. The Iranians have strong influence on them.

In Syria a minority of Alawits (Shia Muslim sect) rule Syria. Ex-president Hafez Assad ruled Syria more than thirty years. Now his son, Bashaar Assad, is in office.

In Lebanon a large segment of the population is made up of Shia Muslims. They are armed and financed by Syria and Iran.

This alliance (Iran, Syria, and associates in Iraq and Lebanon) is seriously dangerous for several reasons:

* Linked geographically
* Rich (Iran alone received more than $50 billion U.S. in oil revenues last year), plus oil-rich Iraq
* Same religious affiliation is in control
* High level of military expenditures. Heavy expenditures on military research and development, especially the Iranian work on nuclear research.
* Participated in several wars
* Police-type control of their countries
* Direct link to North Korea, Russia, China.
* Recently information on agreement between Syria and Russia to establish a Russian navy base in the Syrian seaport of Latikia. Usually this requires providing the seaport area with protection and sharing intelligence information.

The success of Iran, Syria, and associates in Iraq and Lebanon has serious consequences on the Middle East and world peace, such as:

1. Control of the production and shipping of oil in the Middle East
2. Stronger influence on the social and political systems in the Middle East and North African

(MENA) countries, the Arab countries in general, and especially the Gulf Cooperation Council (GCC) countries

3. Serious threat to the safety and security of Israel

4. Strong impact on the stability and peace of the whole world, especially if they succeeded in establishing a strategic alliance with Russia and/or China

This situation is a modern duplicate of the case that prevailed during Almamoun's, son of Haroun Alrashid, Islamic empire (the Abbasids rule). Almamoun had a Persian mother, He was the crown prince in charge of the Persian Islamic areas. He sent his Persian armies to Baghdad to kill and behead his own brother (the Sultan Alamin, son of Haroun Alrashid, had an Arab mother) and replaced him as the Sultan of the Islamic empire.

This is the real threat for the Middle East and the free world today. In a way it started with the emergence of the ALKhomeini rule in Iran and their success in using the Iran-Iraq war and the Lebanese civil war to spread their influence throughout the Middle East, mainly in Iraq, Syria, and Lebanon.

Unfortunately this serious threat is coupled with the hate culture in the Middle East.

The Middle East

The hate culture prevails nowadays throughout the Middle East. To change the current negative conditions in Lebanon, Iraq, and the Middle East the governments should start with the main basic element, the individual human being. **All efforts should be exerted to provide the Arab citizen with real freedom and happiness. A happy person cannot and will not hurt another human being.** To reach this situation, the Arab governments should concentrate on the following issues as a good start:

A. Fight corruption:	The real enemy for the society is the corrupt, dirty official who transfers the limited economic resources of the country to his own or his family's accounts in international banks.
B. Land of laws:	In most local societies, the judicial system reflects the interests of the government officials and their inner circle of relatives, friends, and business associates, the hard-working local entrepreneurs and potential foreign investors are pushed out of the country.
C. The income tax system:	The country's ability to provide good services and social benefits depends on having good revenue. Most of the government revenue comes from income taxes, which could be increased through: - Increasing the tax base, which is the size of economic activities in the country - Increasing tax rates - Improving the policies and procedures to collect the income taxes

D. Developing the financial system in the country The financial markets, institutions, and securities, which in turn increase the funding of the credit facilities to the various economic sectors.

E. The United Nations should establish information centers in the Arab countries. The centers would include documentary films and educational material about the known religions worldwide, especially Christianity and Judaism. Also the United Nations should establish Islamic information centers in Israel and major countries worldwide.

The staff in every center, based in the capital of the country, can go out to various regions in the country to deliver presentations and seminars in schools, universities, and chambers of commerce, and to the members of professional associations in the country. Also it is possible to use one floor in the center as a small museum about the Holocaust. This will help the public to understand the fears of Israel.

F. The Arab countries in 2005 spent on military purposes an amount equivalent to $49.647 billion U.S. I suggest reducing the annual expenditures on military purposes by an amount equivalent to $25 billion U.S., which would be allocated to support a special economic development fund in the Arab countries. So, over a period of ten years, the total amount will be $250 billion U.S. This fund should be managed professionally by experts from the United Nations and international financial companies. The basic purposes of this fund include:

1. Supporting the private sector in the Middle East

2. Supporting the entrepreneurs and the small- and medium-size businesses

3. Coordinating the efforts to gain experience, especially the think tanks, universities, and industrial companies, to develop and support new technologies and business concepts in the Middle East

4. Coordinating with the commercial banks to arrange giving loans to small investors based on guarantees from the fund. Borrowers with no collateral would be able to benefit from such a program. Kindly keep in mind that this idea is already applied in the USA and the kingdom of Saudi Arabia, where the Saudi Industrial Fund manages a program to provide "guarantees" for the small investors (Kafala project).

The peace culture in the Middle East will reduce the brain drain and enable every person to achieve the American dream in every village and city in the Middle East. In this regard I will quote leaders from the area in recent occasions. Sheikh Sabah Al Ahmad Al Sabah, Prince of Kuwait, addressed the Kuwaiti parliament on October 30, 2007. He said,

> *Democracy in Kuwait did not start with establishing the parliament. It started with the early days of Kuwait, - - - - -. The Kuwaiti people gave you their votes because they trust you to achieve their goals of a country where safety, security, justice and equal opportunity for all, you cannot break the law - - - -.*

Also, in a recent meeting in the Vatican between the Pope, head of the Catholic Church, and the Saudi King Abdullah Bin Abdulaziz Al-Saud, they issued a common statement saying,

> *We renew a common commitment to have a dialogue between the various religions and cultures to reach a peaceful coexistence, and stressed on the importance of cooperation between Christians, Muslims and Jews for peace, justice and ethical values.*

In This regard please note that in the history books we learned few things about the Arab occupation of Spain. They discussed the details of the Arab invasion of Spain and the history of the Emirates that they established there. We learned a lot about the Muslims and the Christians in Spain. Recently a TV documentary about the Arab years in Spain mentioned a third group, the Jews, and their role alongside the Christians and Muslims in the scientific and economic developments in Spain during that period. This information about the Jews is missing from most of the history books in the Middle East, as if they never existed. But the fact is that the Jews lived in Spain. Also they lived in the Middle East before Islam. **The peoples of the Middle East, before Islam, consisted of Jewish tribes, Christian tribes, and the nonbelievers.**

The history books and few movies refer to the Jews here and there as individuals who opposed Islam and Muslims from the early years of Islam. It is used as a basis for the hate culture against the Jews throughout the past 1,400 years till today.

Nobody bothered to mention that maybe the Jews were hurt and angry because someone was telling them negative things about their religion.

Please note that during the last few years several incidents happened in Europe that were considered offensive acts against Islam and Muslims, such as the regulations imposed in the French public schools, not allowing the girls to have their heads cover. Also it stressed not having any religious symbols in the public schools, even the cross symbol.

At that time demonstrations by Muslims were held in several countries worldwide. People were angry because of a small incident that involved a small number of girls. Let us imagine the situation 1,400 years ago when the Jewish and Christian tribes were informed that they had to pay taxes because they were Jews or Christians living in a Muslim empire. Moreover, today, if the USA or the European countries decide to impose taxes on Muslim immigrants or visitors simply because they are Muslims—even if the tax amount is one U.S. dollar per person—imagine the reaction of all Muslims. Undoubtedly they would be hurt and angry. Let us go back 1,400 years ago and consider the position of the Jewish and Christian tribes in the Middle East. Maybe we will have a better understanding of the wars and conflicts between the Jews and the Muslims during that period.

Also maybe we will understand the difference between the Jewish people and the crusaders. The crusaders were Europeans. That is why they returned to Europe later. But the Jewish tribes lived in the Middle East. At a certain point, they were not strong

enough and lost their ground. Today they are strong enough to keep their ground.

Another problem in our attitudes about the Middle East is the way some Arabs consider the USA and the American presence in the Middle East unwelcome. Kindly bear with me and assume that the American people decide next week that they want to keep their sons and daughters safe at home. So the USA decides to take out of the Middle East all their bases and military forces. Also the White House indicates that America will not interfere in the Middle East anymore.

I have no doubt at all that within a few months there will be a new map for the countries in the Middle East. Somalia and Iraq will be nice, good places to live in compared to what most of the countries and cities in the Middle East are expected to be in the absence of the USA military and political presence.

The basic players are:

1. Israel. Its military capabilities and FEARS are known.

2. Iran-Syria and associates in Iraq and Lebanon. Their announced goals and hidden agenda???

3. Turkey. Frustrated because the doors of Europe are closed. So what about the OTTOMAN Empire revisited?

4. Every single country on planet EARTH. (Except the USA, because the Americans are fed up with the Middle East.)

I hope that the ones who enjoy blaming the USA for every problem in the Middle East start appreciating the blessings of having the USA.

I am sure of this. One does not need much time to figure out that we need to appreciate the importance of having the USA as a strategic partner. Moreover, we need to fight the hate culture in the Middle East.

The situation in the Middle East is critical, no doubt. Difficult decisions should be made by all involved. There are no easy solutions. Unfortunately it seems that most of the parties are reluctant to change. After the 1973 war, President Sadat initiated a peace process. At that time the Israelis were open to having the Palestinians included in the peace process. Several sources talked about the possibility of having a

Palestinian state in the West Bank and Ghaza. The response from the Arab side was negative.

Most of the Arab leaders were in office for twenty years or more (Saddam Hussein, Yaser Arafat, Hafez Assad). So they were still negotiating with the '50s and '60s in their minds as a background. Later, in the early '90s, after the Madrid peace conference, more than half a million Israelis from the "Peace Now" movement demonstrated in Tel Aviv, calling for peace. Again, most of the Arab leaders were still living in the '60s. Moreover, they were in office from 1990 to 2007, while in Israel more than seven prime ministers changed over that period. In every government change, the new prime minister goes more to the right. And the "Peace Now" demonstrations reduced to few thousands participants.

The Middle East is known in the media as the land of the "lost peace opportunities." The situation reached a critical point. The leaders in the Middle East need a training course on managing change. In fact, we need this course in every school and university in the Middle East. The reluctance to change is expected to result in another NAKBA (Forced immigration of the Palestinians). The situation in Ghaza is getting worse and Israel will not allow another Holocaust involving the Jewish people. The Arab politicians and media are using the hate culture against the Christians and Jews and building up the dreams and illusions of the extremists in Ghaza and the West Bank. Please take a minute to analyze the situation there. How long is this escalation in anger, hate, and violence expected to continue? One, two, three years? At a certain point, the whole situation will explode. One party (Israel) is prepared and well armed, while the other party is relatively weak. When the situation explodes, who will be able to push the other party out of the area?

My impression is that the American administration is trying to keep all parties aware of the serious situation. The American soldiers are sacrificing precious blood in Iraq in their effort to stabilize the situation and stop the Iran-Syria Persian Islamic empire. But the American and free-world effort is not enough alone. It should be supported fully by the moderate Arab leaders and people throughout the Middle East. Both parties should stand up against the emergence of this Iran-Syria new Persian Islamic empire.

Unfortunately the hate culture is strong. It goes back hundreds of years, and everyone remembers the negative issues. I read once that when Prophet Muhammad died, he had his shield mortgaged to a Jew. Obviously Muslims, Christians, and Jews were living together in the Middle East. Also, they were conducting business with each other. I do not see why the present should be different. **Even now most of the Arab government officials and the media still cannot see clearly that Iran-Syria and its associates in Iraq and Lebanon are the enemy and the real threat to them and the whole world. The Iranians used thousands of twelve-year-old Iranian Muslim children to walk through the mine fields to clear the way for the regular Iranian military forces during the Iran-Iraq war. Also, they used chemical weapons, political assassinations, and international terrorism. The hate culture directed toward Israel—along with the corruption, oppression, and all other aspects of the hate culture—cloud the judgment of the Arab officials and the public.**

The absence of common sense in the Middle East will result in having a large number of small, fragile religious and tribal countries or emirates, as indicated by the Iraq situation.

The whole civilized world may face a shortage of oil. But certainly the Arab leaders and the peoples of the Middle East will live in war, agony, and pain for years to come.

This alliance between the USA and a peace-culture Middle East is essential. But this alliance will not fly with one wing only (the USA). **The peace culture in the Middle East is a must.** The Arab leaders should work hard to stop building up this hatred toward the Christians and Jews and should instead exert serious efforts to fight oppression and corruption and to spread the peace culture to every country to achieve the American dream of liberty, justice, and happiness for every person and every family in the Middle East.

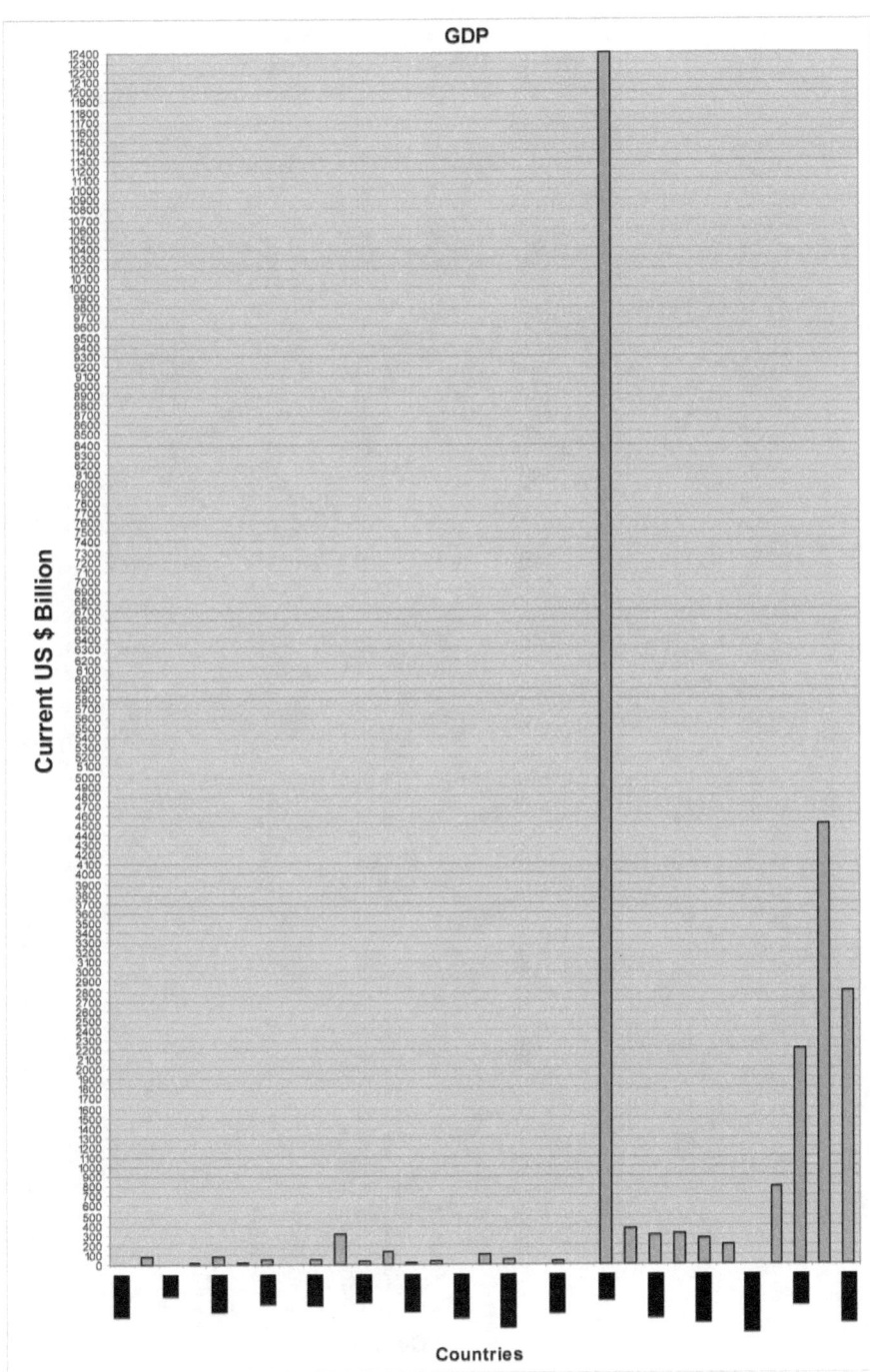

Foreign Direct Investment

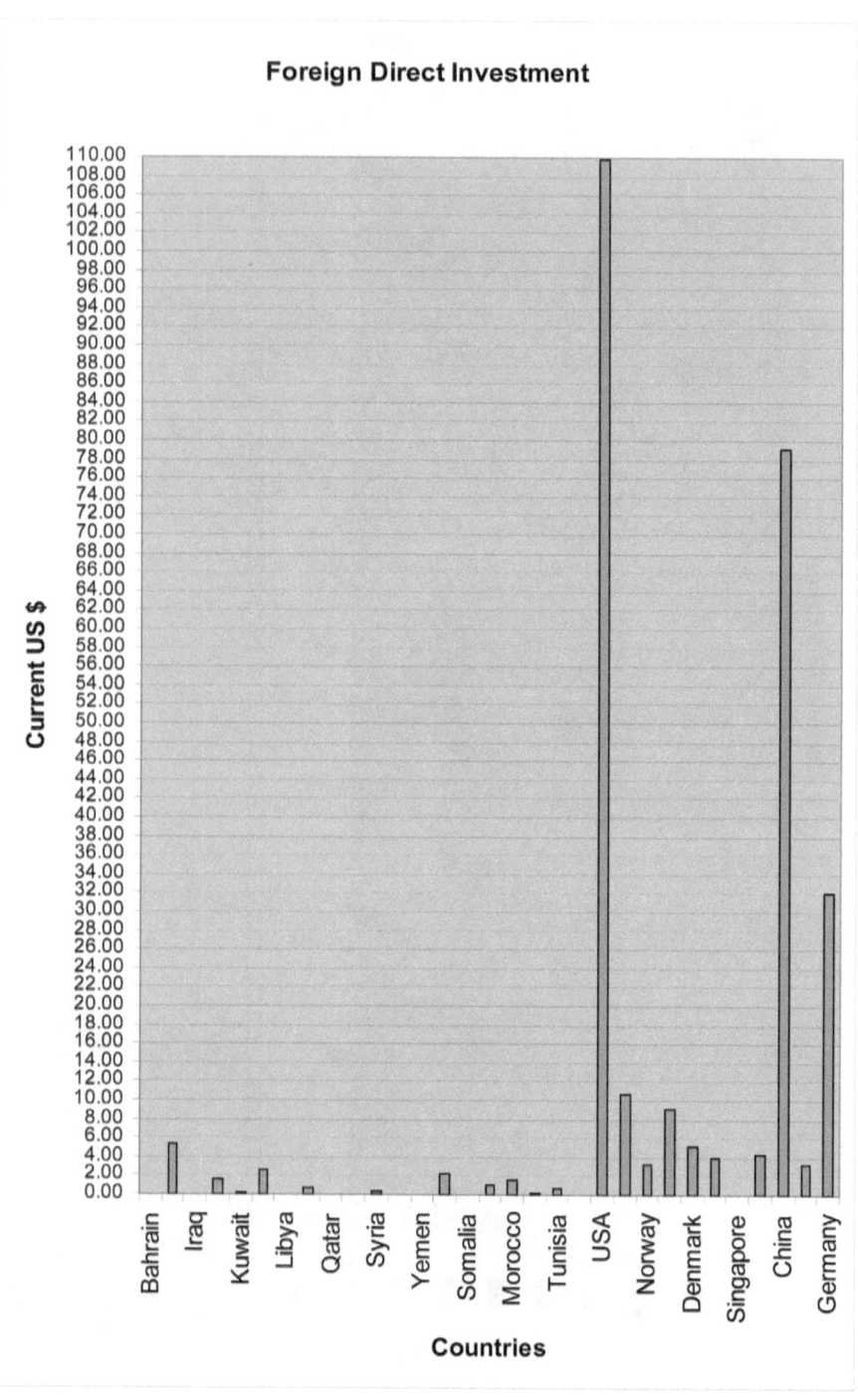

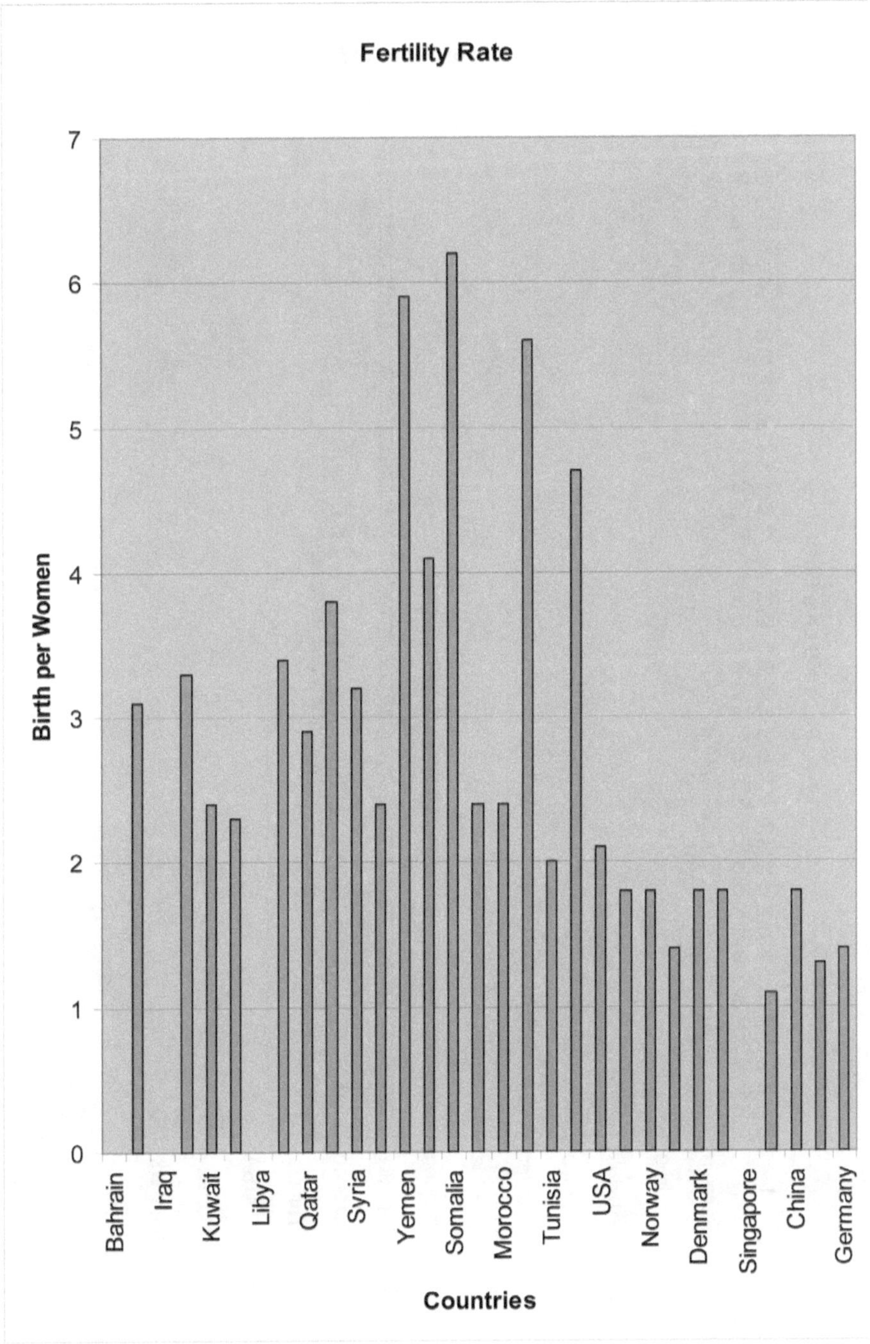

Fertility Rate

Birth per Women

7

6

5

4

3

2

1

0

Bahrain
Iraq
Kuwait
Libya
Qatar
Syria
Yemen
Somalia
Morocco
Tunisia
USA
Norway
Denmark
Singapore
China
Germany

Countries

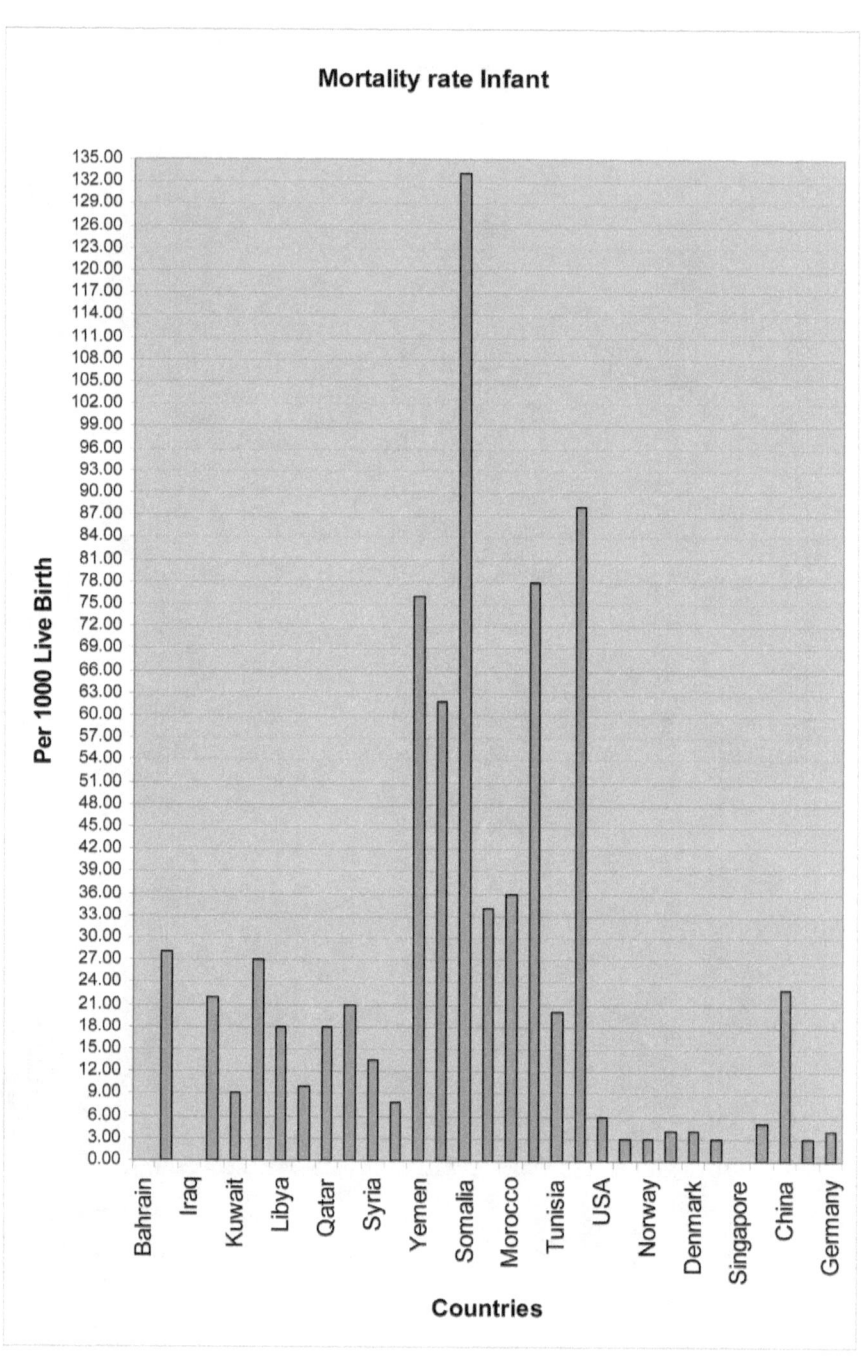

Mortality rate Infant

Per 1000 Live Birth

Countries

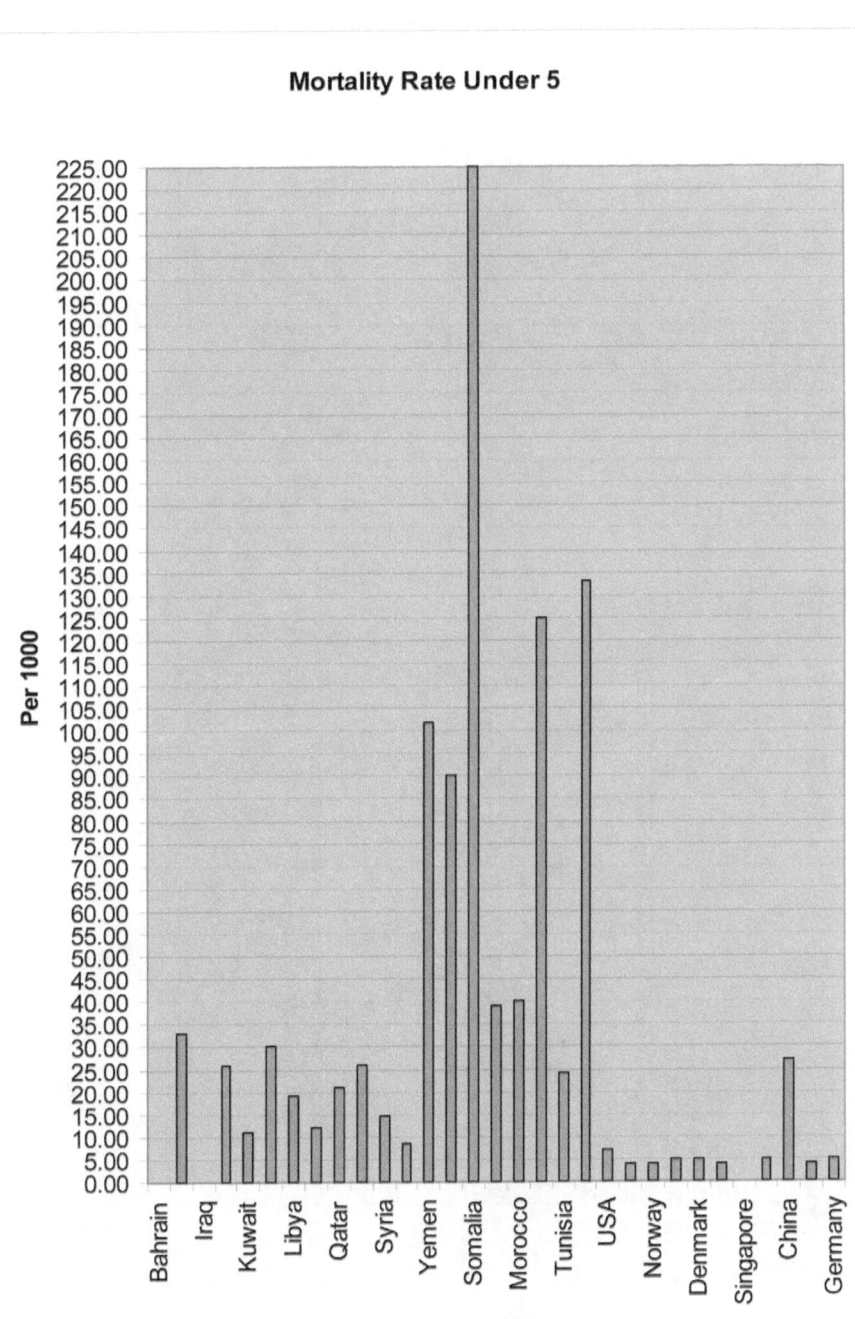

Mortality Rate Under 5

Per 1000

Countries

Ease Of Doing Business

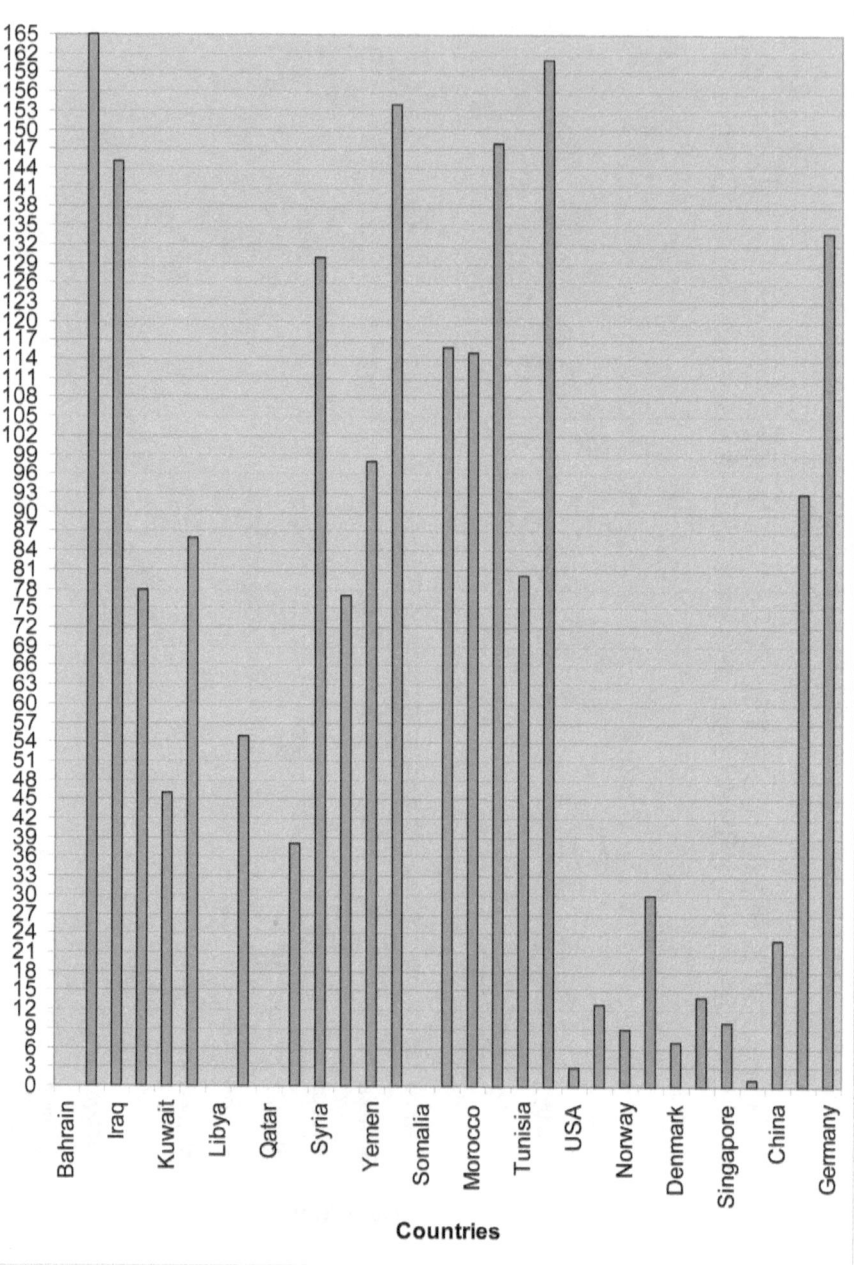

Countries

Starting a Business

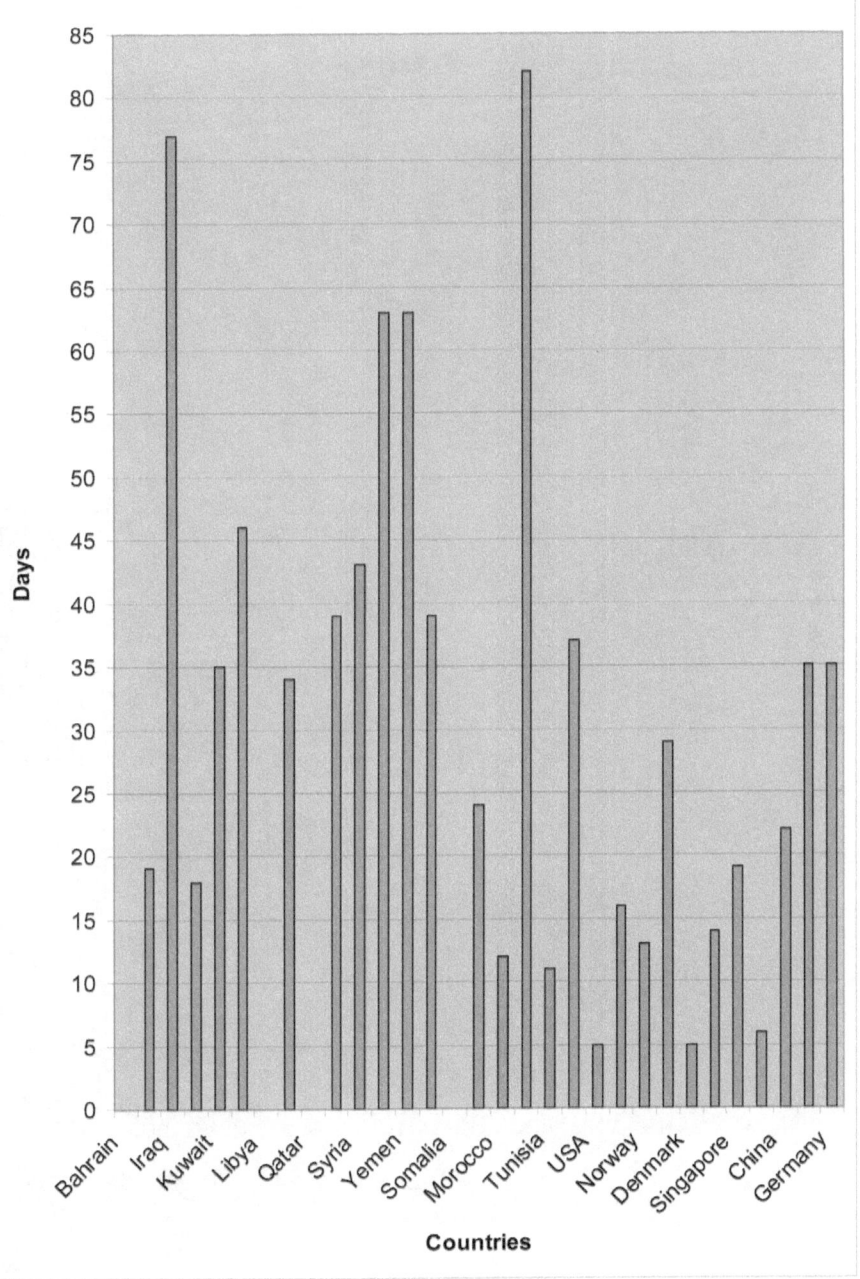

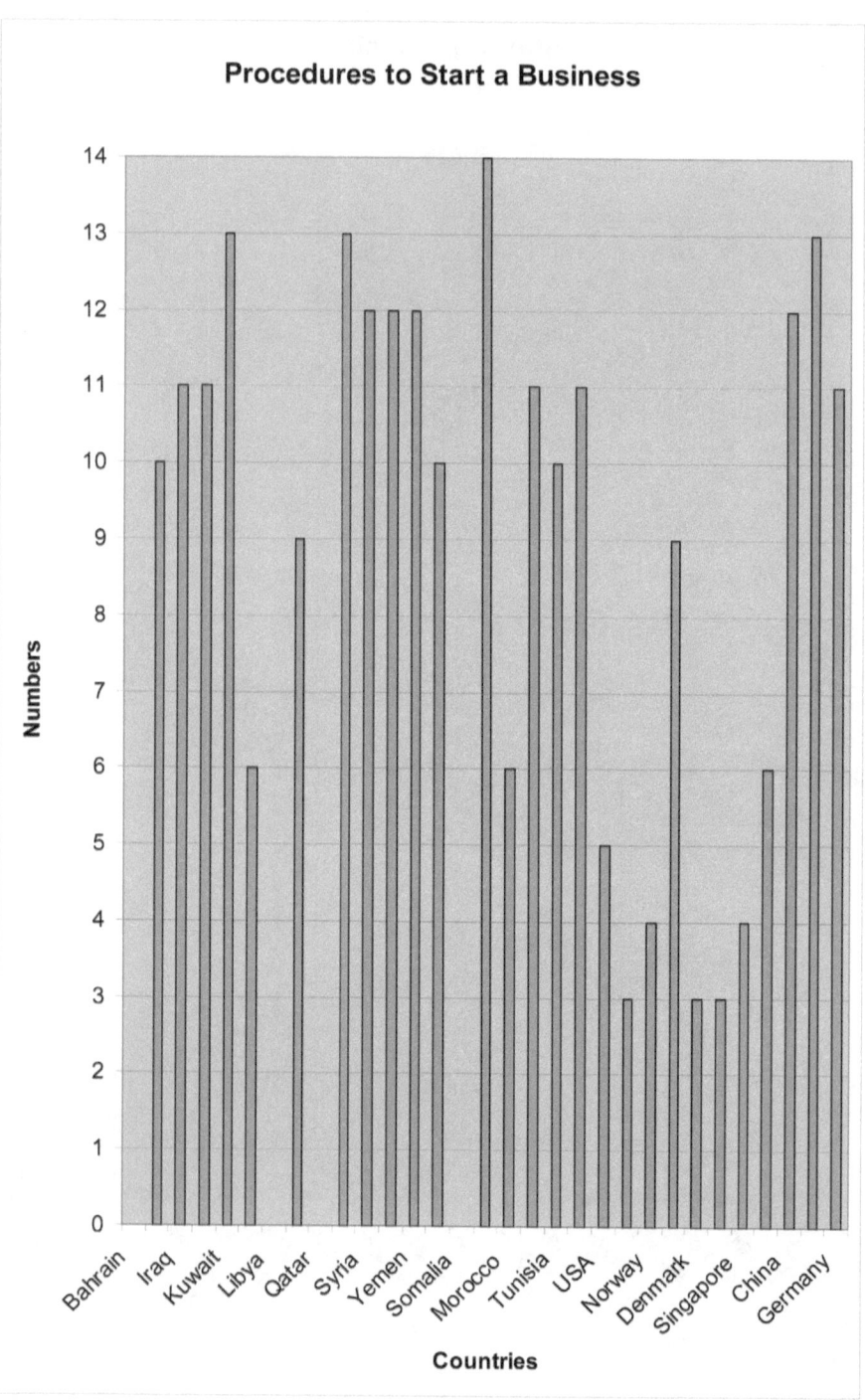

Procedures to Start a Business

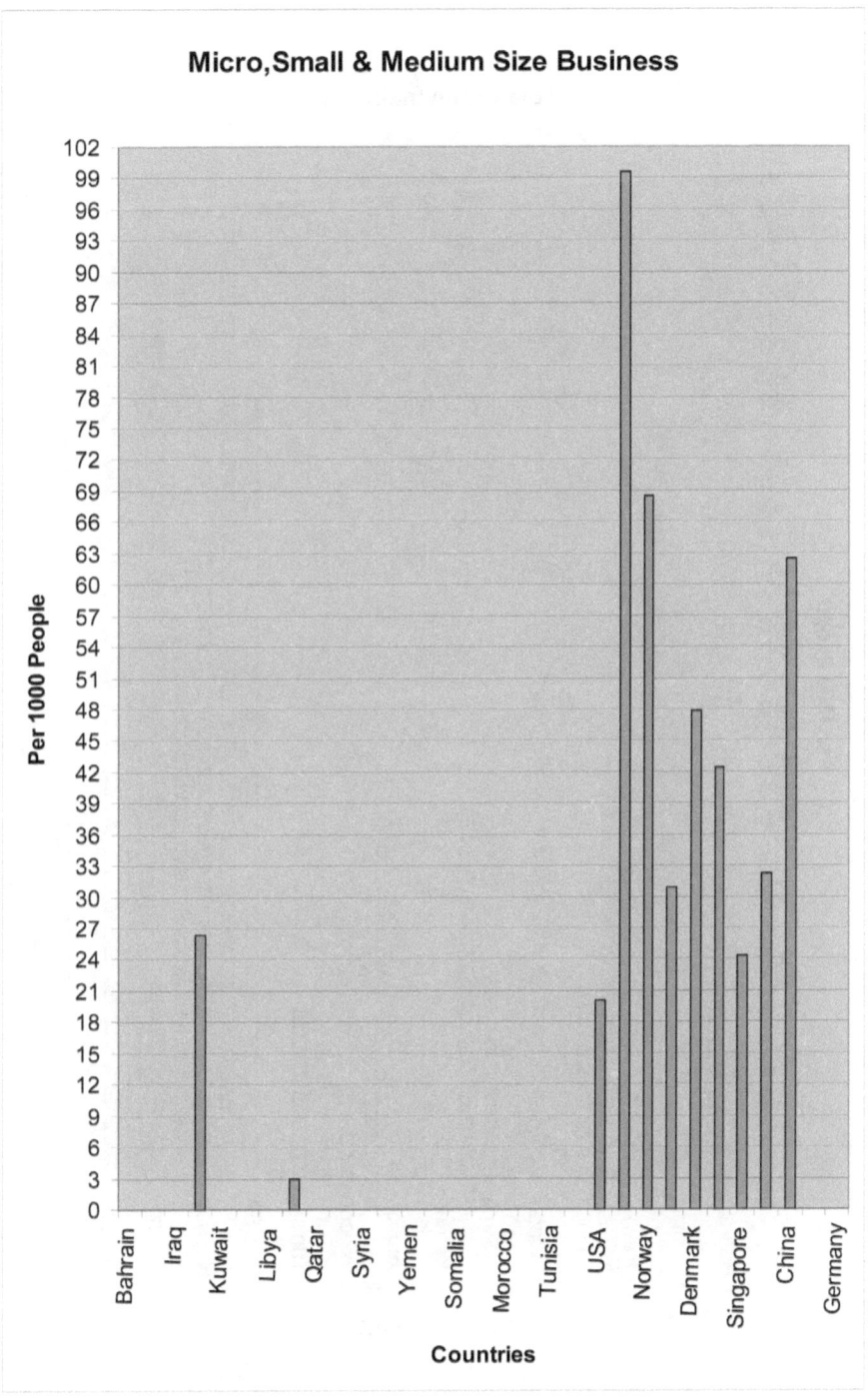

Micro,Small & Medium Size Business

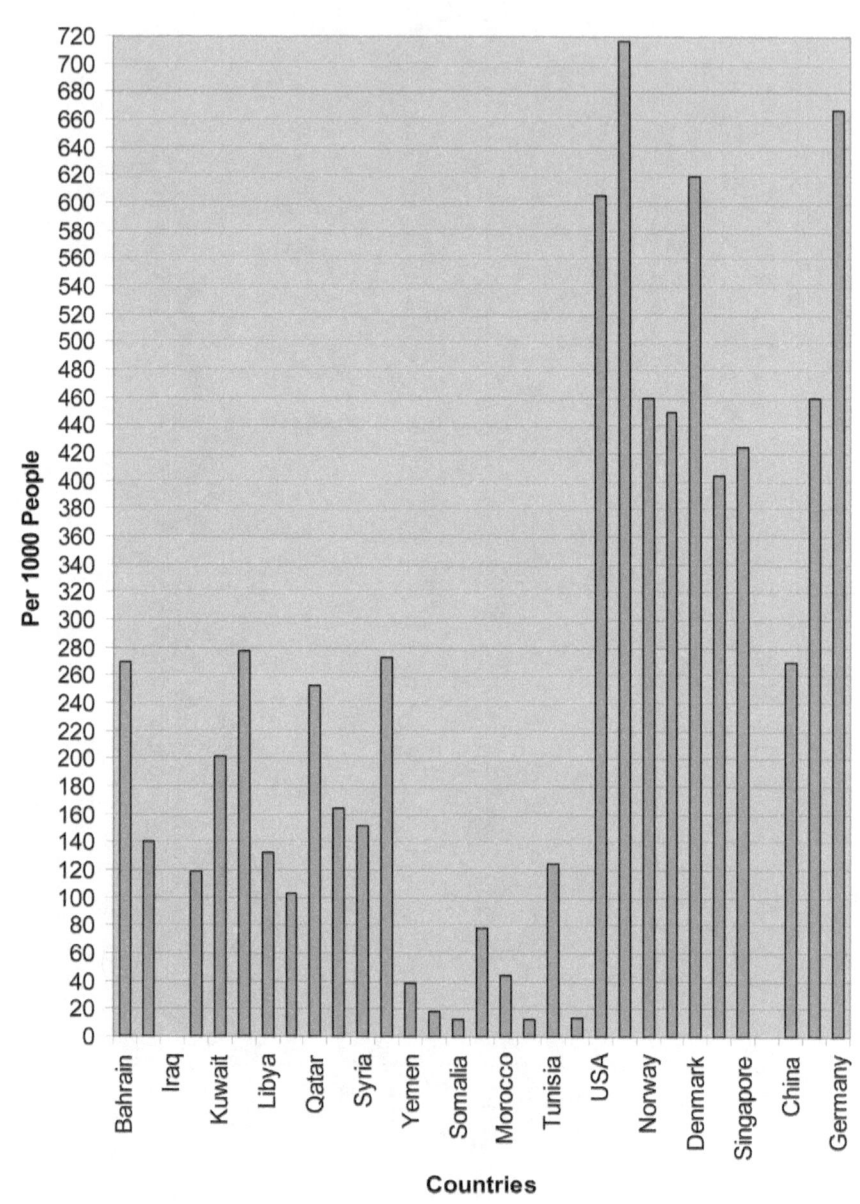

Telephone main Lines

Per 1000 People / Countries

Mobile Subscribers

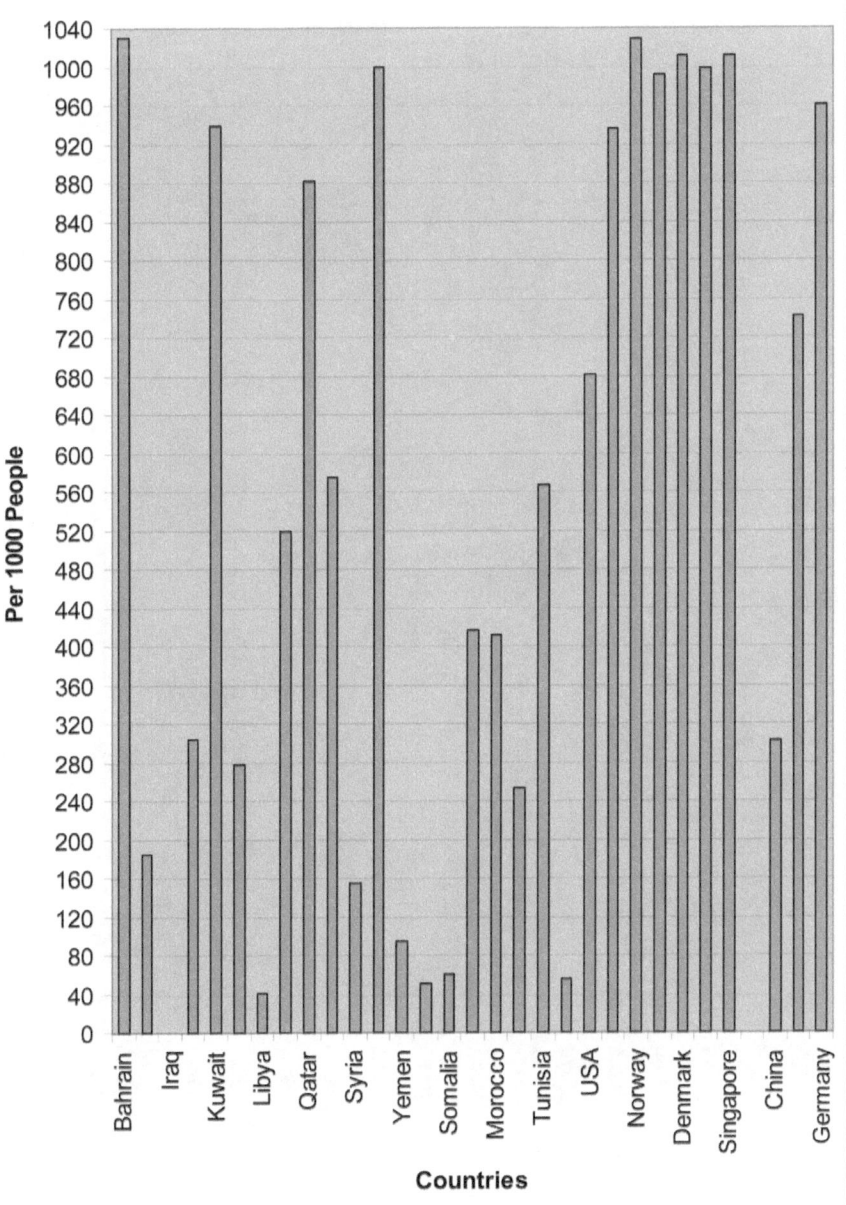

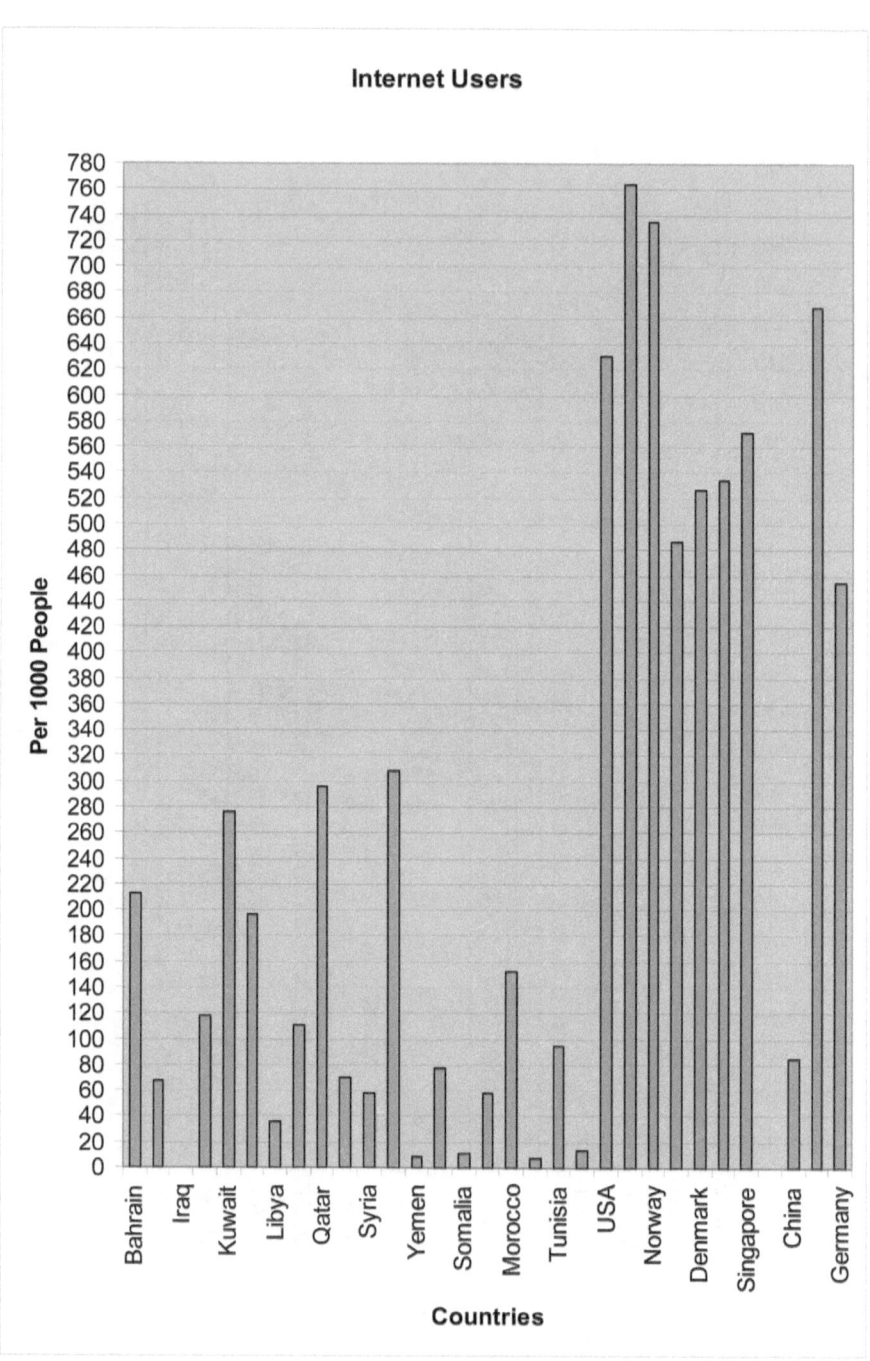

Internet Users

Per 1000 People / Countries

Bahrain, Iraq, Kuwait, Libya, Qatar, Syria, Yemen, Somalia, Morocco, Tunisia, USA, Norway, Denmark, Singapore, China, Germany

Personel Computers

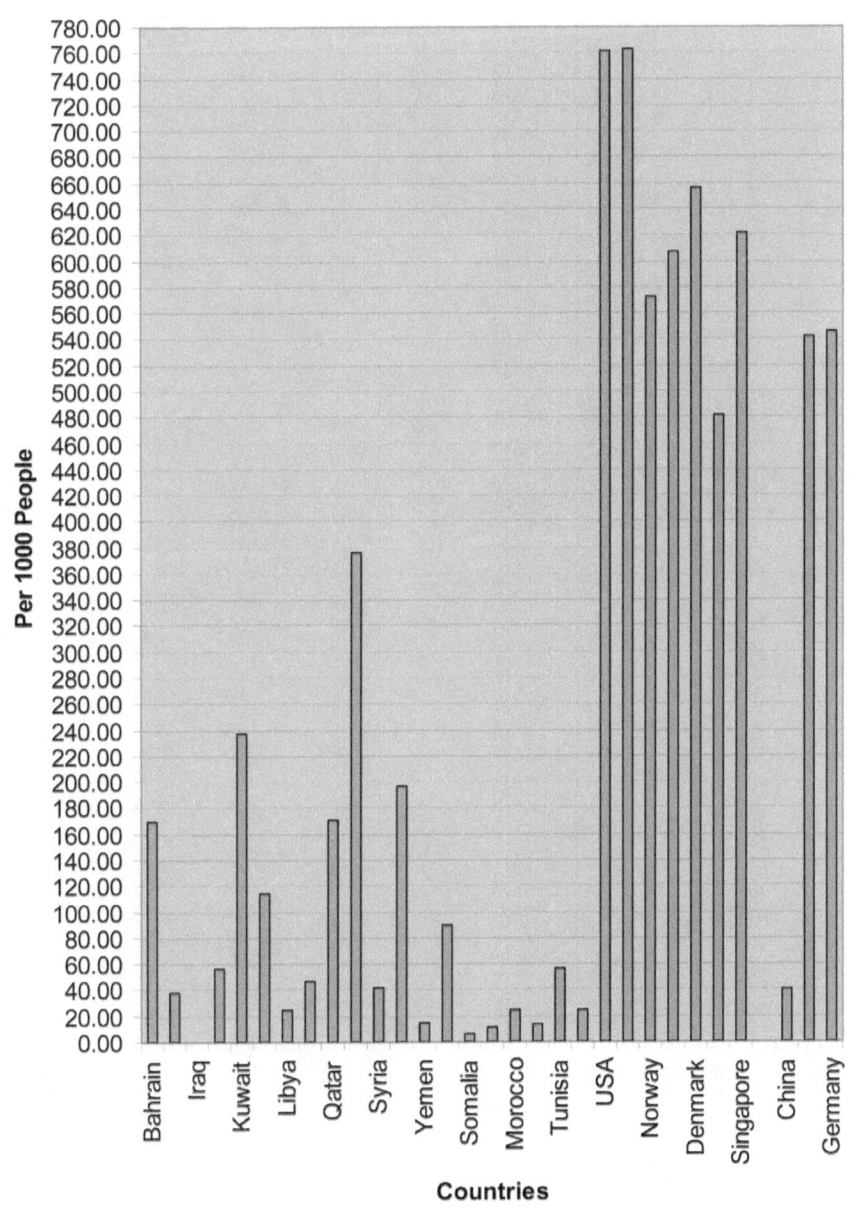

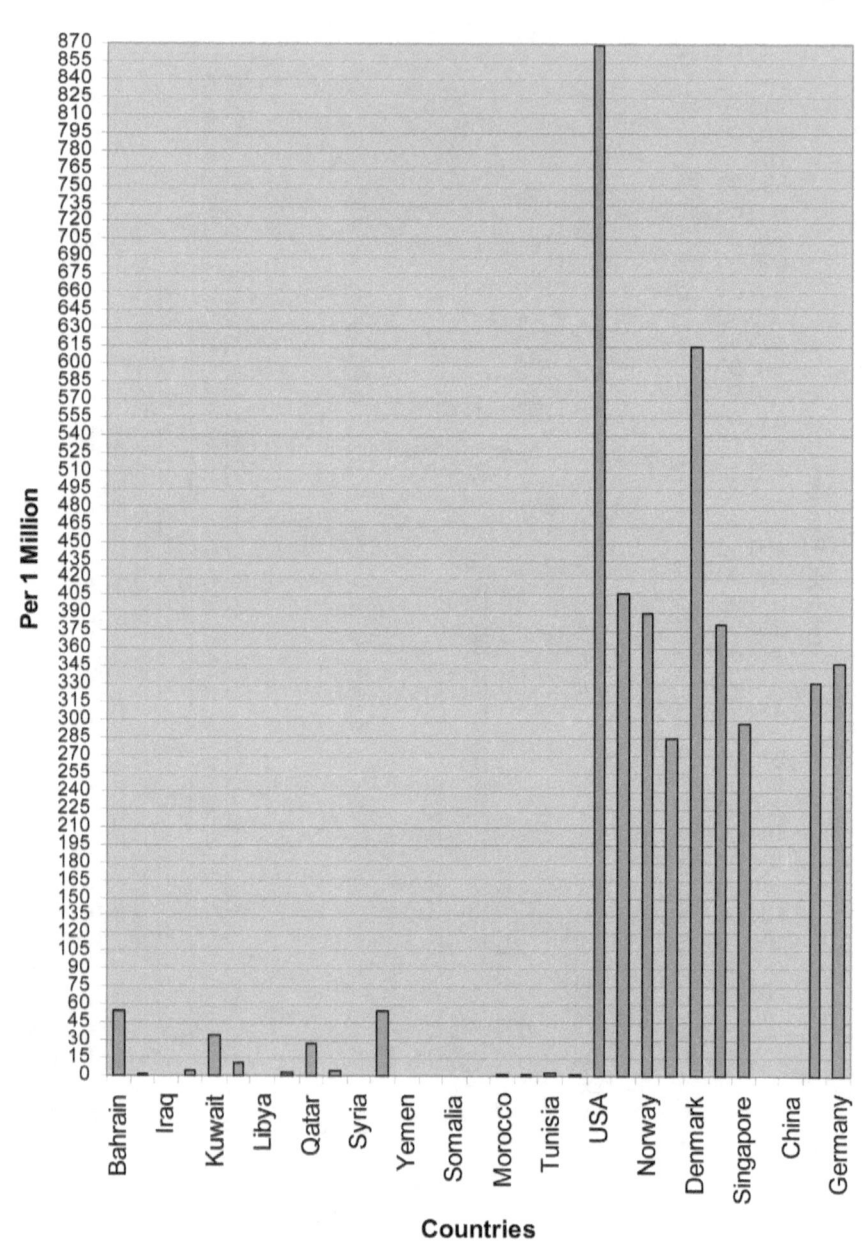

Secure Internet services

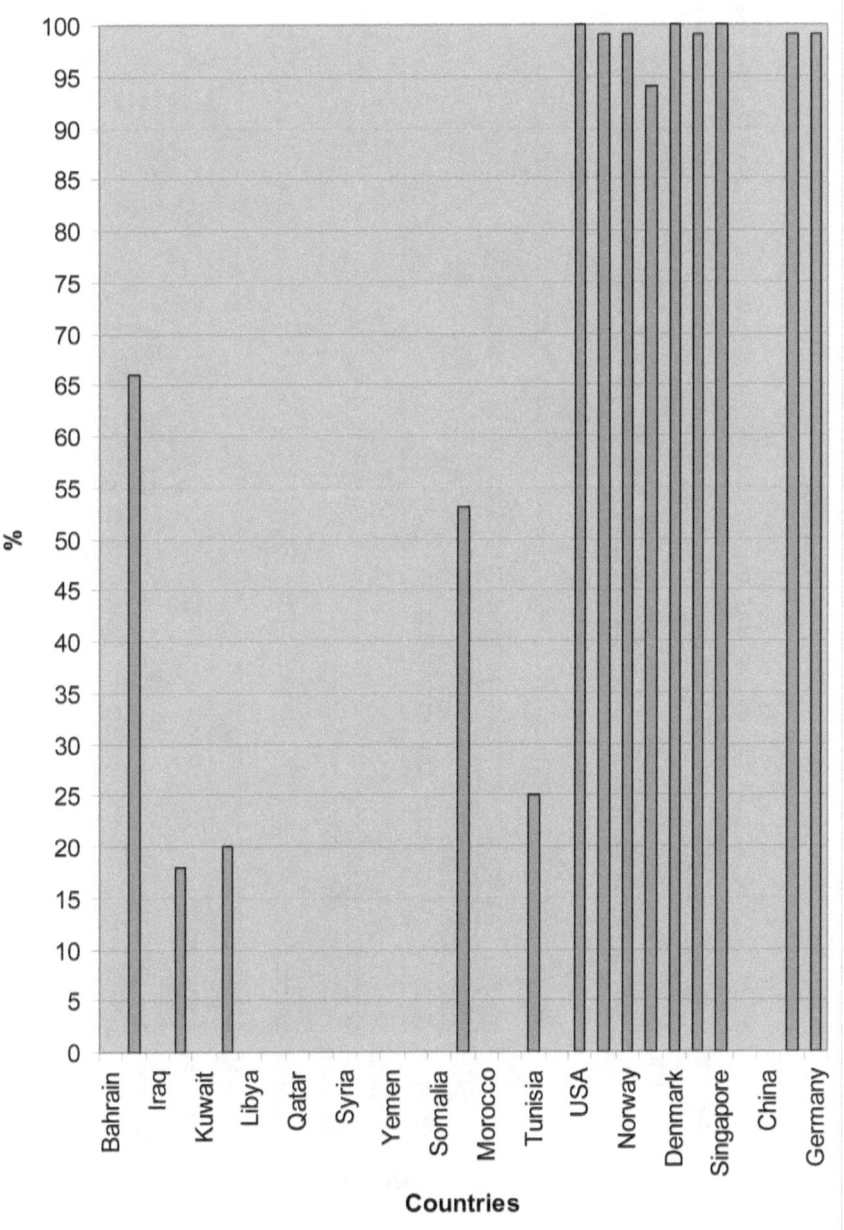

Schools Connected to te Internet

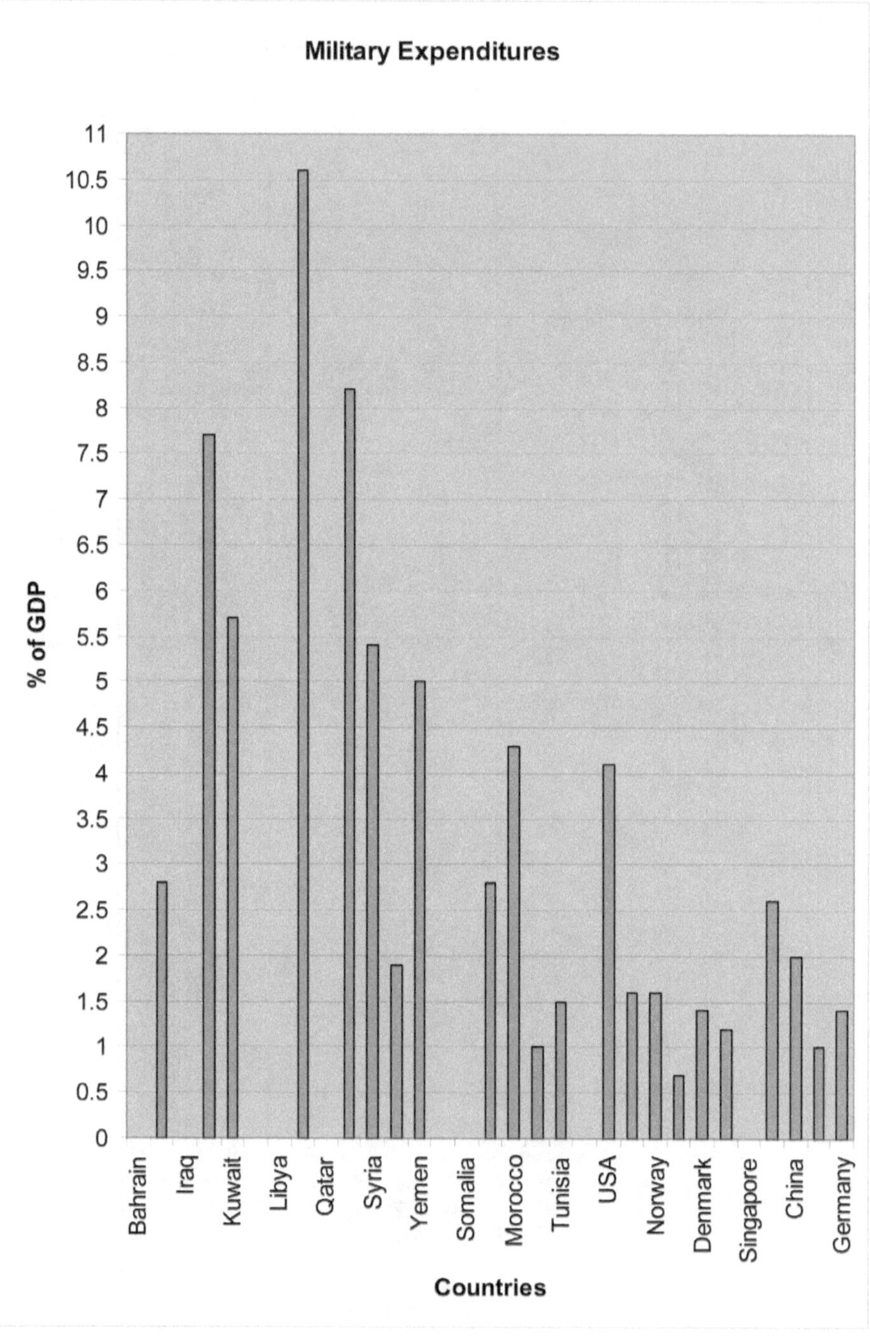

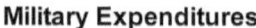

Military Expenditures

% of GDP

11
10.5
10
9.5
9
8.5
8
7.5
7
6.5
6
5.5
5
4.5
4
3.5
3
2.5
2
1.5
1
0.5
0

Bahrain
Iraq
Kuwait
Libya
Qatar
Syria
Yemen
Somalia
Morocco
Tunisia
USA
Norway
Denmark
Singapore
China
Germany

Countries

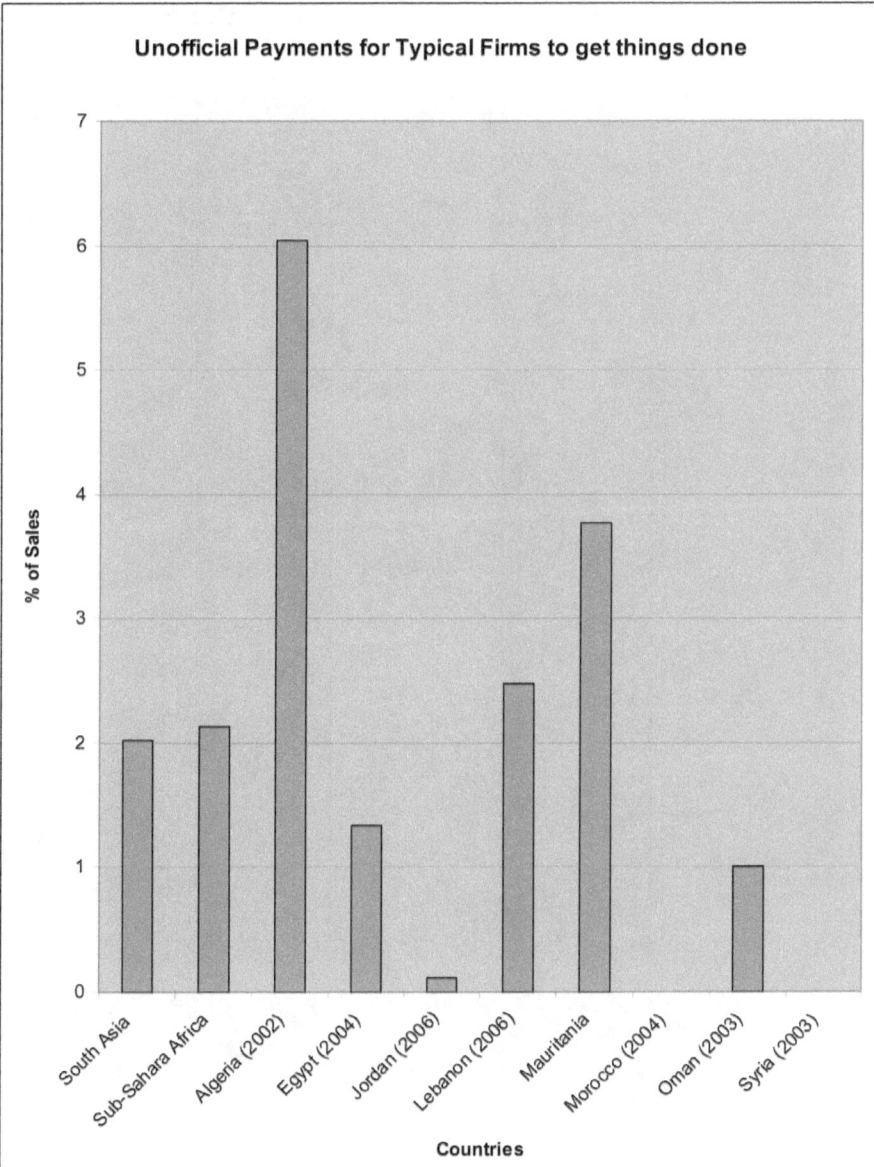

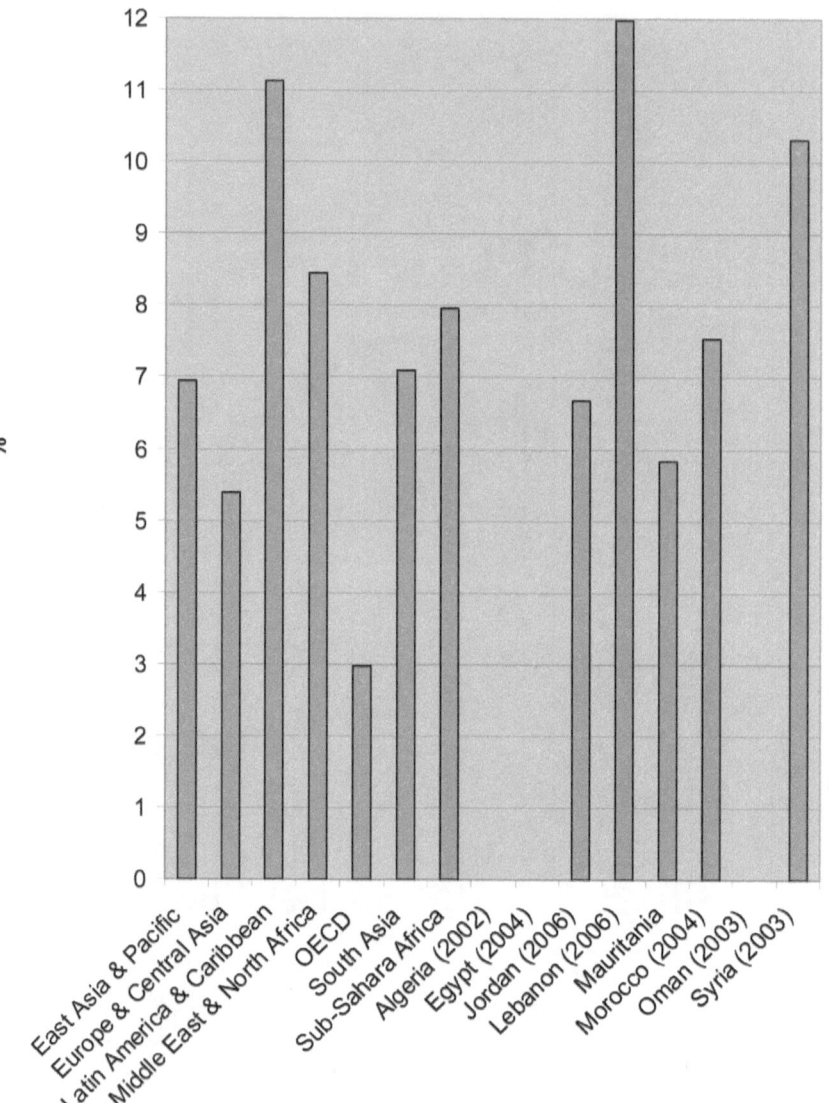

Senior Management Time Spend In Dealing With Requirements of Government Regulations

%

Countries

East Asia & Pacific
Europe & Central Asia
Latin America & Caribbean
Middle East & North Africa
OECD
South Asia
Sub-Sahara Africa
Algeria (2002)
Egypt (2004)
Jordan (2006)
Lebanon (2006)
Mauritania
Morocco (2004)
Oman (2003)
Syria (2003)

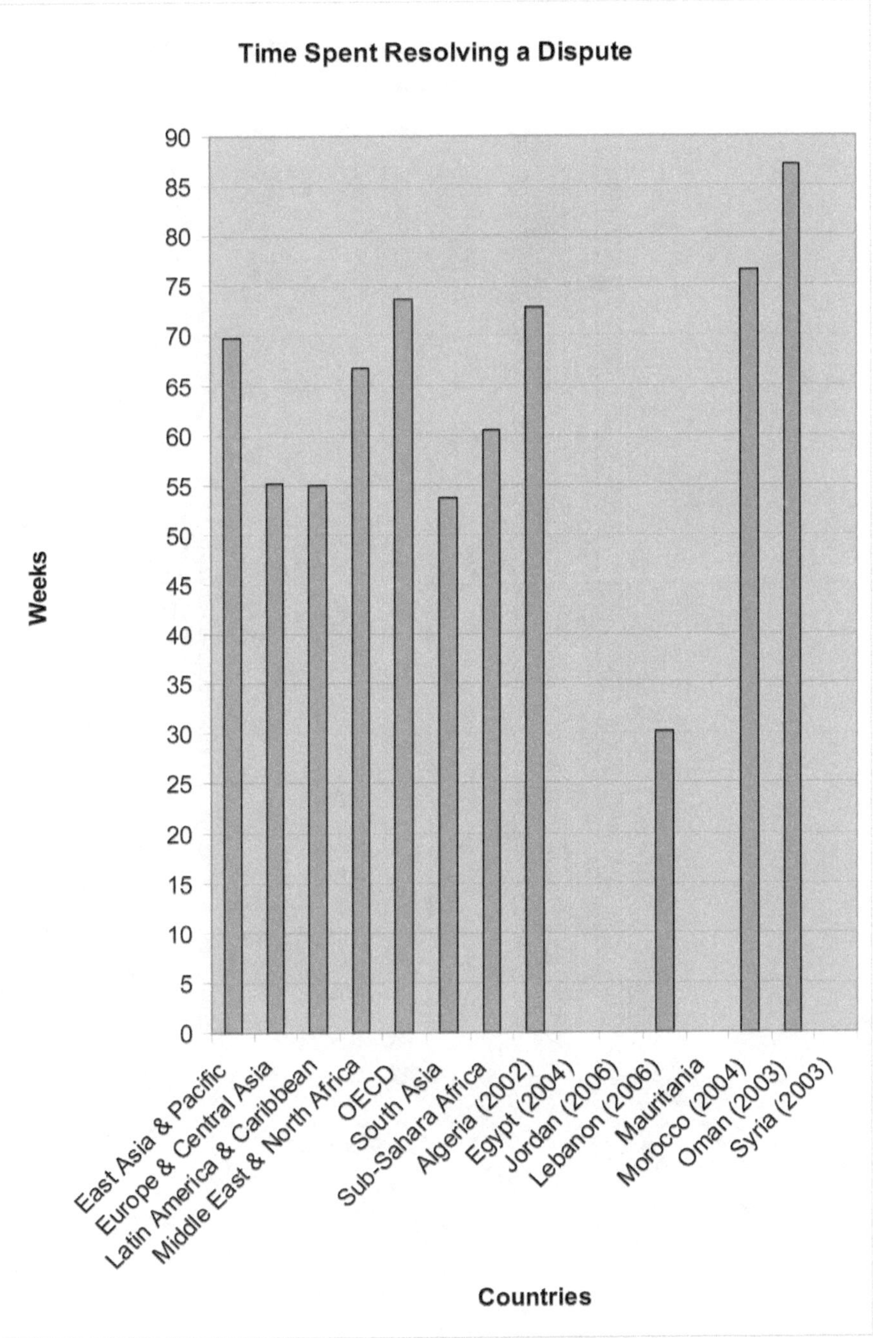

Time Spent Resolving a Dispute

Weeks

90
85
80
75
70
65
60
55
50
45
40
35
30
25
20
15
10
5
0

East Asia & Pacific
Europe & Central Asia
Latin America & Caribbean
Middle East & North Africa
OECD
South Asia
Sub-Sahara Africa
Algeria (2002)
Egypt (2004)
Jordan (2006)
Lebanon (2006)
Mauritania
Morocco (2004)
Oman (2003)
Syria (2003)

Countries

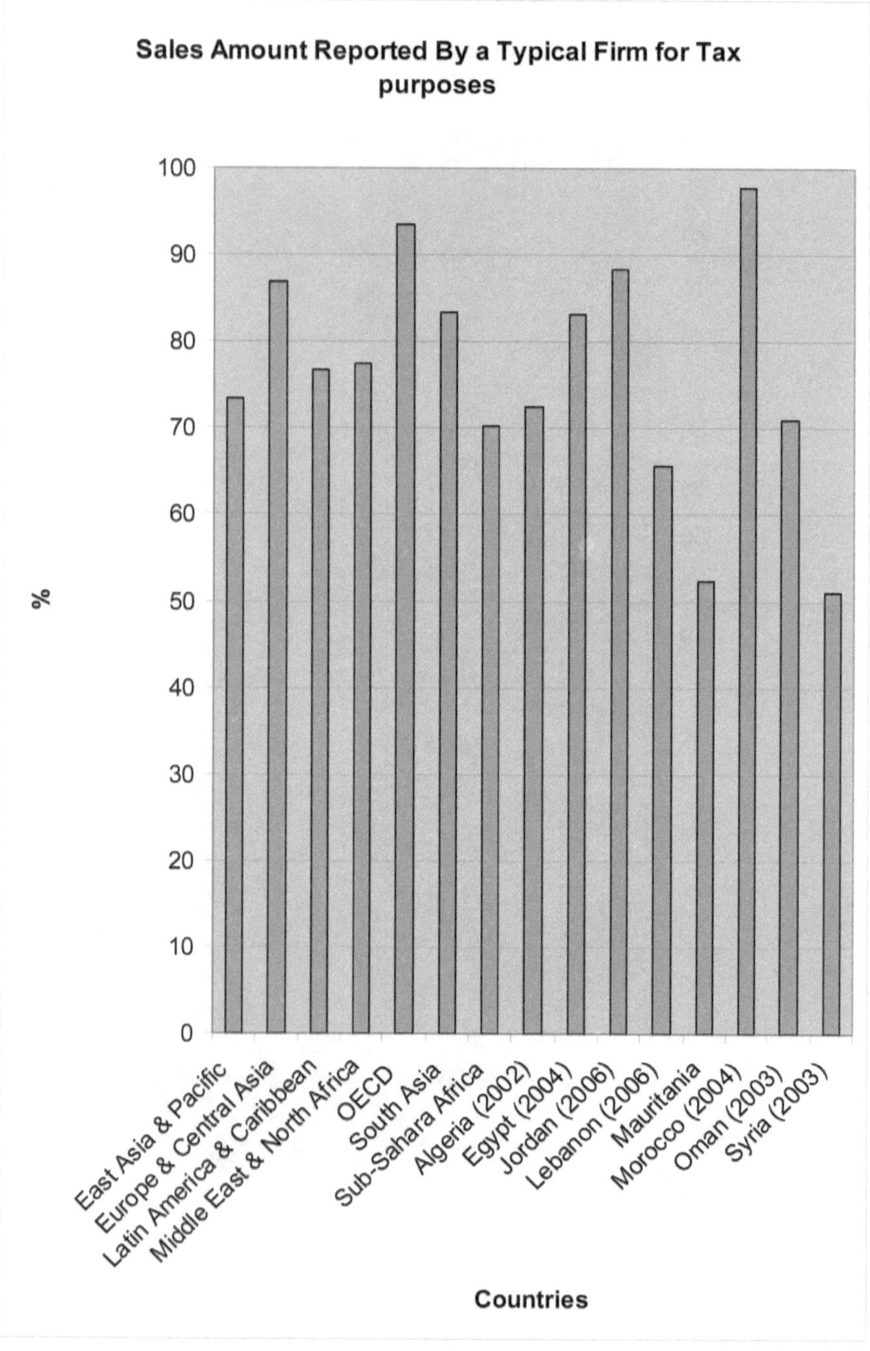

Sales Amount Reported By a Typical Firm for Tax purposes

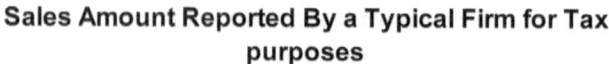

Countries

82

Delay in Obtaining an Electrical Connection

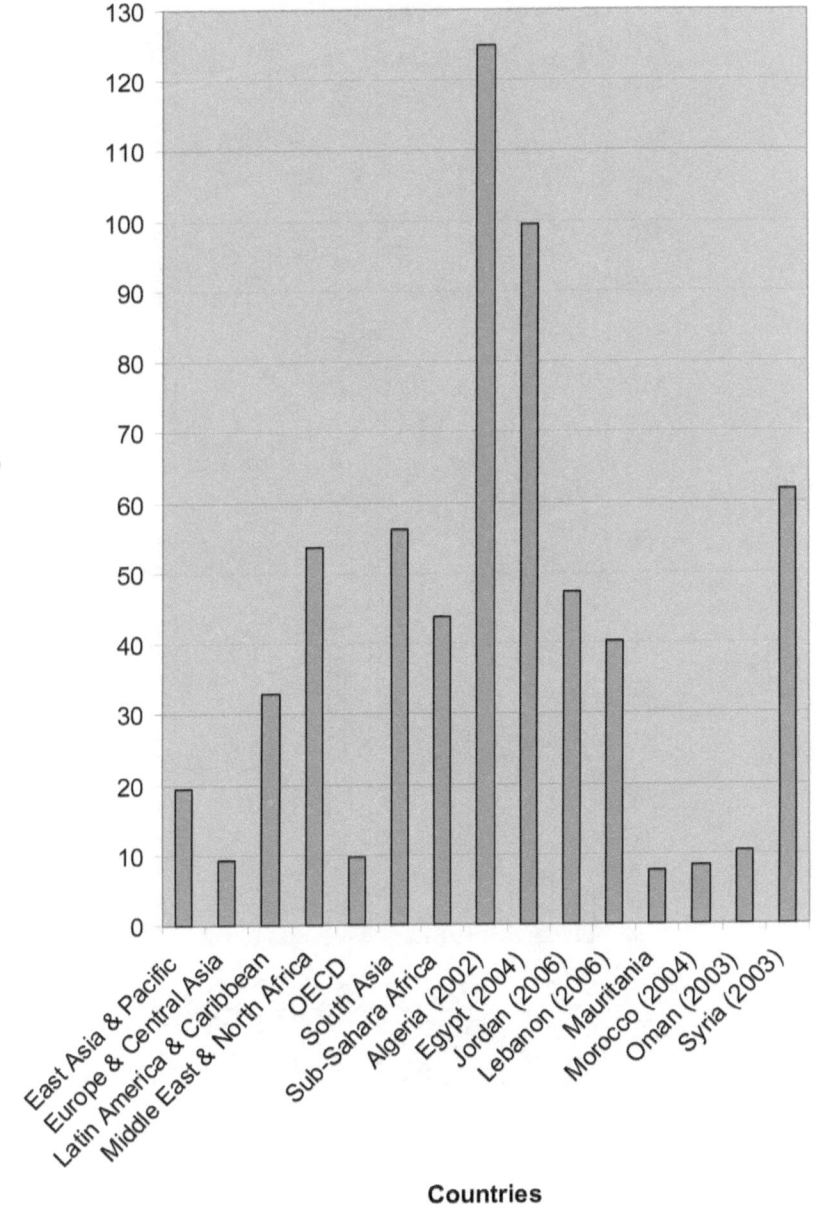

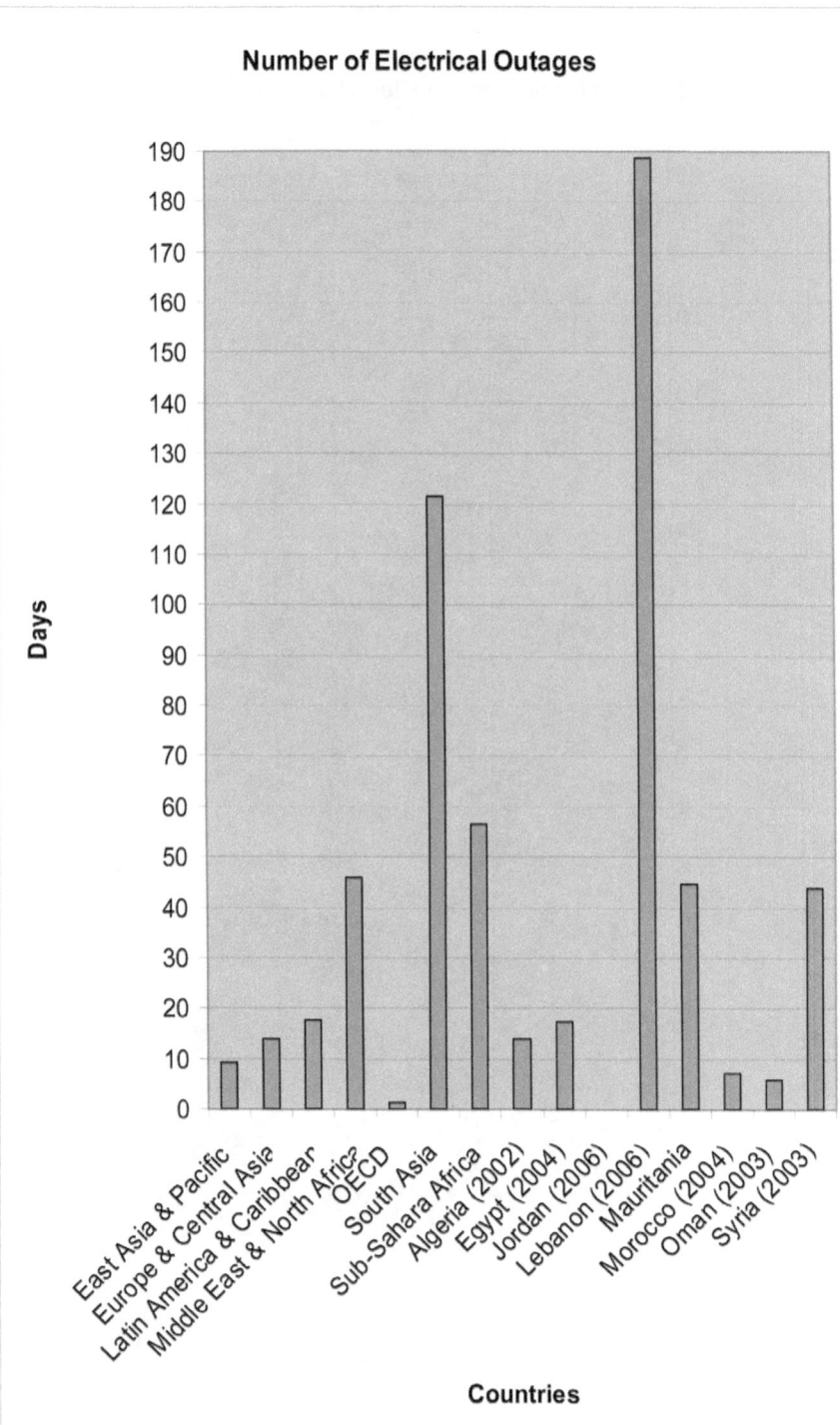

Number of Electrical Outages

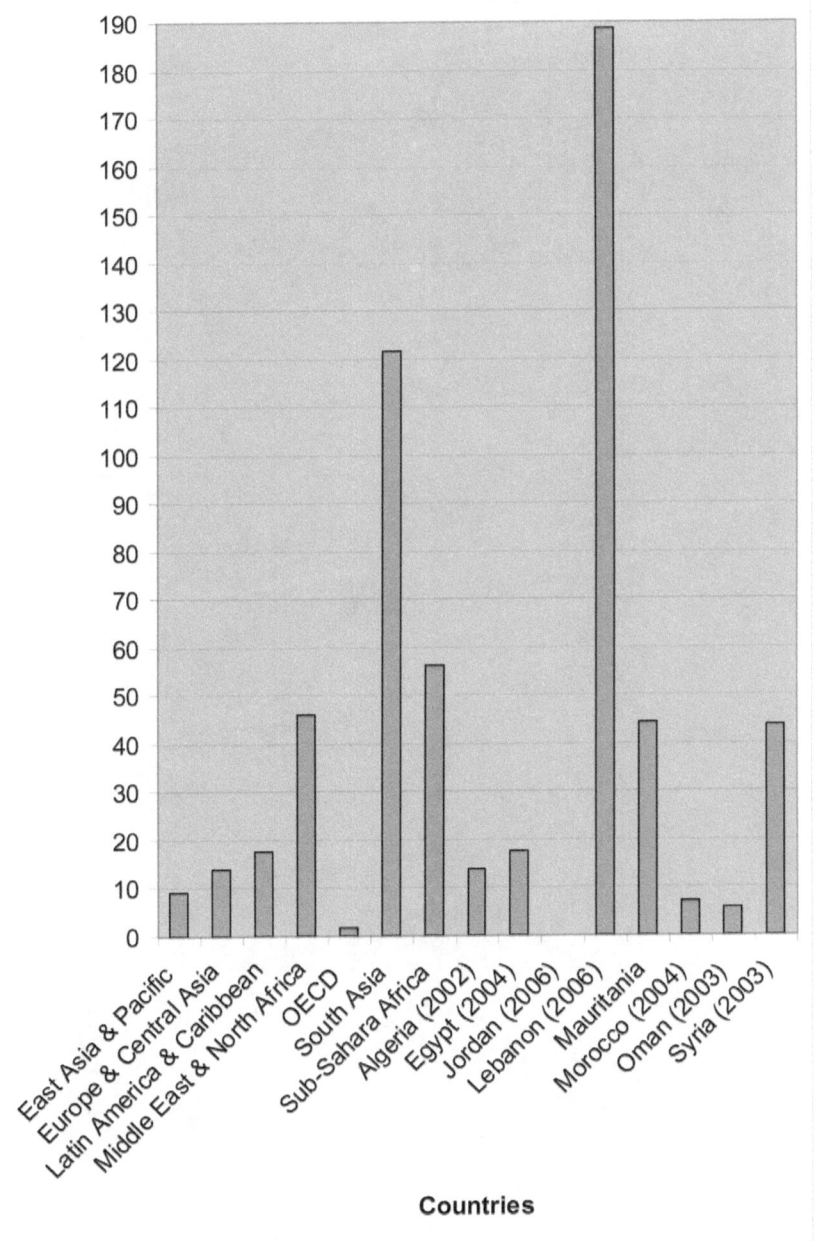

Value Lost Due to Electrical Outages

% of Sales

Countries

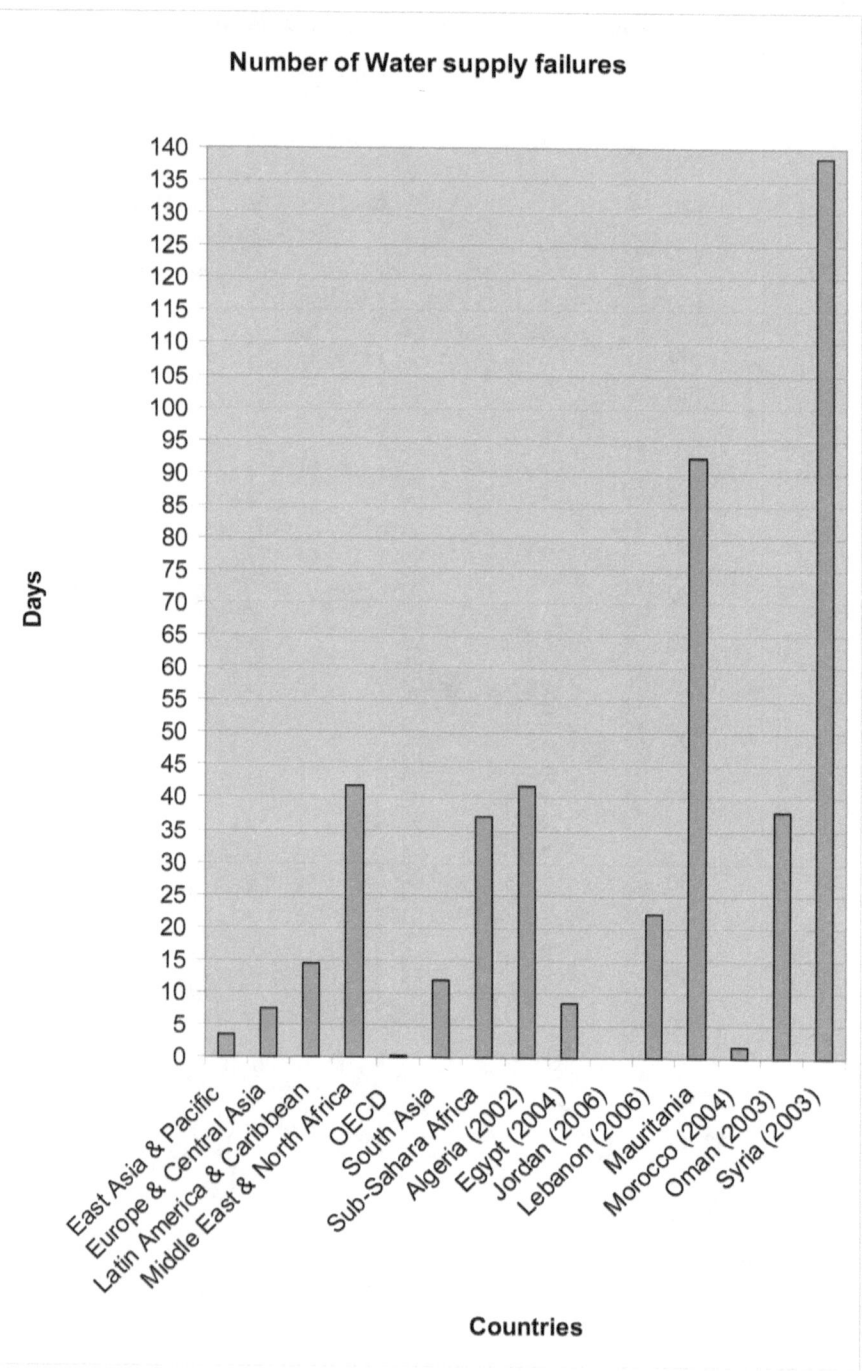

Number of Water supply failures

www.ingramcontent.com/pod-product-compliance
Lightning Source LLC
Chambersburg PA
CBHW031246280526
45784CB00004B/1745